Celebrating Quiet Artists: Stirring Stories of Introverted Artists Who the World Can't Forget

Prasenjeet Kumar

Published by Prasen Publishers LLP, 2016.

CELEBRATING QUIET ARTISTS: STIRRING STORIES OF INTROVERTED ARTISTS WHO THE WORLD CAN'T FORGET

First edition. June 10, 2016.

ISBN: 978-8197187933

Written by Prasenjeet Kumar.

Table of Contents

Introduction

How many times have you heard this?

"You/your child just day dream/dreams. Your child doesn't socialise enough. How is he/she going to survive in this competitive world?"

Believe me, I too have heard a lot of such comments when I was in school. These came from teachers, friends and well-wishing family members. Some were benign, but quite a few were caustic—and they really hurt. These comments, or advice as they were cloaked as, were passed on to my parents as a cause for concern.

And in my teenage years, I really thought something was wrong with me.

After all, eminent personalities like Steven Spielberg, Agatha Christie, J.K. Rowling, Leonardo Da Vinci, Amitabh Bachchan and the like were all extroverted and outgoing, unlike me. Right?

No. Absolutely wrong.

They were quiet. And introverts. Like me. Like you.

And yet, their contribution is so well known. Just imagine a world WITHOUT them. What would it be like? Without Harry Potter. Without Mona Lisa. Without Hercule Poirot. Without Inspector Vijay. Without E.T.

So if these artists were really introverts like you and me, how did they leave such an indelible imprint on this world? Did they learn to become fake extroverts? Did they practise skills of socialising? Did they learn to talk non-stop?

Hell no.

They stayed true to themselves. Their inner selves. And they used their most precious power of introversion—of day-dreaming—to create fantastic characters, music or pieces of art.

Yes, day-dreaming is indeed a very powerful tool. Especially when you are a creative person. Without a rich imagination, NO art is possible. Period.

And they used the other strength of quietness—Persistence. They never gave up on their dreams. No matter what the obstacle was. Or how severe the setbacks were.

And they kept practising their art—till it became perfect or sort of "perfect."

In the coming pages, you'll see how many of these quiet artists were scalded with confidence-shattering incidents. Professional tragedies. Personal tragedies. Health issues. Suicidal tendencies—you name it.

Yet they rose from the ashes like the Phoenix bird. Powerfully but quietly.

Like a Quiet Phoenix.

I read a lot of books but have never come across a book that celebrates day-dreaming.

I wrote this book, therefore, to specifically celebrate the rich imagination of introvert artists. And their beautiful, magnificent and awe-inspiring creative endeavours.

The book shatters another myth. That artists cannot make a living doing what they love doing.

Yes, the path may be difficult. But if you use your quiet strength or strengths, as I may say, no one can stop you from succeeding in your chosen career.

I hope you will enjoy reading these uplifting stories as much as I enjoyed writing them.

Prasenjeet

Chapter 1: A Quiet Unschooled Girl Becomes the Most Read Novelist in History

In November 1961, the world woke up to a series of intriguing murders. In almost all cases, the victims had shown similar symptoms. These included: hair loss, lethargy, numbness, black-outs, slurred speech and general debility. Experts discovered that all victims were poisoned by thallium, which is a highly toxic, colourless, odourless, and tasteless liquid. Its biggest "advantage" was that it was slow acting. So you could put thallium into water, food or drink and see its effect only after a week.

So who had committed these crimes and why?

The "credit" went to a gentle 70-year lady who claimed, "Give me a decent bottle of poison and I'll construct the perfect crime."

The lady was, in fact, the unlikeliest person to commit those unspeakable crimes. She only wrote about them, in a new genre that had become a rage as "murder-mysteries." In all, this quiet woman wrote 91 books that sold over 2 billion copies. Publishers also translated her books into forty-five languages making her the most read novelist in history.

And this is when the lady was almost unschooled. She had some tutoring at home, but only after 9 years of age. So she taught herself by reading books.

When she was just five, her father Frederick learnt that there was almost no money left in his estate. He tried to find a job, but, as the lady recorded in her autobiography, "like most of his contemporaries," he "was not trained for anything." He died when he was just fifty-five. For the little girl and her mother dinner was often rice pudding.

The little girl had no companions to speak to, as her sister and brother, Madge and Monty, were more than a decade older. She also had no schoolmates because she attended no school. Her social world comprised of the family's three servants. So she spent a lot of time with her imaginary friends: kings, kittens, and chicken. Later, as an adult, she was so painfully shy that she could not even enter a shop on her own.

Her older sister, Madge, was an excellent writer though not by profession. She declared once that the little girl who loved to read detective novels so much could not write one. With books from authors like Edgar Allan Poe and Arthur Conan Doyle, this genre was then just becoming popular. The young woman took on the challenge and wrote her first detective novel just to prove her sister wrong.

The rest as they say is HISTORY.

So who was this woman and what was her story?

To be sure, as all young women of her era, this lady too had not thought of a career. She wanted a husband, and that was it!

But as someone who couldn't publicly reveal her emotions, writing provided great comfort to her. She believed she could express herself better in writing than in speaking.

During the First World War, this lady volunteered to serve as a nurse. Later she worked in the pharmacy at the University College Hospital, London. This was where she could pick up all her knowledge about poisons. For example, she learnt about the use of thallium as a poison from the UCH Chief Pharmacist Harold Davis.

Her descriptions of poisons in novels turned out to be so precise that they sometimes even saved lives. In one incident, a woman from South America suspected that her acquaintance was being poisoned by his young wife. In another, a nurse spotted the symptoms of thallium poisoning in a nineteen-month old baby in Qatar. Both had reached their conclusion after reading the lady's novels and both turned out to be correct.

On the flip side, critics accused her of giving ideas to would-be murderers. In an incident in France, a fifty-eight year old office worker murdered his aunt using atropine eye drops. During investigation, the police found a novel of this famous mystery queen with the relevant passages on atropine underlined. It was clear that the novel had served as an inspiration for the murder.

So have you guessed who this woman was?

Yes, she was the legendary, one and only, **Agatha Christie.**

Her novel about thallium poisoning was **"The Pale Horse."**

And yes, she was a quiet, and a very private person.

In her autobiography, she admitted:

"*I don't like crowds, being jammed against people, loud voices, noise, protracted talking, parties, and especially cocktail parties, cigarette smoke and smoking generally, any kind of drink except in cooking, marmalade, oysters, lukewarm food, grey skies, the feet of birds...*"

Born in 1890, Agatha Christie grew up in a large house in Torquay, a seaside resort in Devon, England. Her mother Clara, wrote poetry, and was interested in Unitarianism, Theosophy, and Zoroastrianism. Agatha adored her and spent hours poring over her jewellery and ribbons.

Agatha had a vivid imagination and all of her characters were imaginary. She primarily wrote to entertain herself. In a notebook, she used to work out her plots. She would make a list of possible victims and culprits and picked up combinations that pleased her the most. She loved playing a game with her readers keeping them guessing who the culprits were.

Agatha created two well-known detective characters in her novels. One was Hercule Poirot, a retired Belgian police officer. He sported a funny moustache and pointed shoes and took pains to proclaim in a French accent that he could speak perfect English! His investigating style involved exaggerating his foreignness so that the culprits took him less seriously and blabbered on without a thought about the consequences.

The inspiration for this character obviously came from Agatha's childhood spent in France where she had learnt to speak French fluently.

The other was a woman called Jane Marple who had the mind "like a sink" and made a rule to see the worst in everyone. She was the opposite of Poirot. Looking like a "sweetly bewildered old lady." Marple would often knit and murmur platitudes. This would—like Poirot, put the suspect off-guard and help get Miss Marple to the bottom of the mystery.

Typically the plots involved—maybe eight or nine people—in a small place: a snowbound train, a girls' school, an English country house, and then—oh no! A body drops. Who did this? And why, and how?

A detective would soon arrive requesting that no one should leave, please. He would then question the people, one by one. In the end, he would gather everyone around and reveal the verdict, announcing the name of the murderer along with the motive and the method.

The culprit would almost never protest. Occasionally, he would go off and commit suicide. But as a rule, he would have no problem confessing: "God rot his soul in Hell! I'm glad I did it!" He would then exit quietly, under police escort.

Agatha is best known for her detective novels but she also published six romance novels (under the pen name of Mary Westmacott), two collections of poetry, one children's book, two autobiographies and some plays. Her play *The Mousetrap* is the longest running show in the world. It premiered in 1952, but it has been playing at St. Martin's Theatre at the West End, London since 1974.

Another play *Ten Little Indians (And Then There Were None)*, first appeared on stage in 1943 and still is a great production around the world even today.

When Agatha was just a teenager, her first novel, *The Mysterious Affair at Styles*, was published, two years after it was submitted as manuscript. Her first contract stipulated that she write five more novels. Instead Christie produced 82 detective novels and 91 books! Her most successful novel, *Ten Little Indians (And Then There were None)*, has had over 100 million sales. *Publications International* lists the novel as the 7th best-selling novel of all time.

To be sure, Agatha was a product of her times. The period between the First and Second World Wars is considered the golden age of the detective story. Housewives would buy such books with their groceries. The genre was so popular that almost any murder-mystery stood a good chance of getting a publishing contract.

That fact was no doubt in Agatha's mind when she took a plunge in this sector. Her greatness, however, lay in the fact that she could offer her readers what they wanted; basically a "puzzle mystery" in which the author challenged the reader to guess who the culprit was before the end of the book.

Agatha hated violence. So in her novels, the detective never ever draws a gun, even when someone acts dangerous. In fact, the detective doesn't even carry a gun. Bystanders may feel free to wrestle the villain to the ground. But if there be no bystanders, the detective could manage the situation by squirting soap water into the murderer's face!

Believe it or not.

Experts have come up with all kinds of explanations for Christie's popularity and for the general enthusiasm for the detective genre in her time. According to Auden, the fundamental appeal was religious. He explained that, at least in Protestant countries, crime solving appeared to relieve "our guilt vicariously."

Others have noted how the interwar years suffered from terrible political upheavals. In that milieu, Christie's stories may have reassured people that disruptive forces lay not in the social order but just in one bad person, who could be caught and removed.

But whether the appeal of the detective story lay in restoring order or not, nothing could diminish Agatha Christie's popularity. She received the British award C.B.E. in 1971; and the Nicaraguan government put the fictional Poirot's face on a postage stamp!

As Kathryn Harkup explains in the book, "A is for Arsenic: The Poisons of Agatha Christie," there was no match to Agatha's use of chemistry driving her plots. Her mastery over poisons, that provided the pacing, was absolute. She knew of each poison's strengths, weaknesses, and idiosyncrasies. So Arsenic's solubility in hot water, atropine's bitter taste, phosphorus's propensity to endow its victims' intestines with an eerie glow, were all skilfully used to permit Miss Marple or Monsieur Poirot to solve the mystery.

In her choice of poisons, Agatha even remembered to use Hemlock, which no one had "used" since the days of Socrates! Ricin, which looks like castor-oil seeds, had no track record as a murder weapon. But that didn't deter Agatha from using Ricin on four members of the same household in "The House of Lurking Death." This was years ahead of her time. The next publicly reported use of Ricin happened in 1978 when the Bulgarian dissident Georgi Markov was assassinated in London using a Ricin-tipped umbrella.

To be sure, Agatha's familiarity with poisons reflected the comfortable co-existence that the society in those days enjoyed with chemicals like strychnine that most patent tonics used. Anyone could buy opium openly without any question. All gardeners used potassium cyanide as an insecticide freely.

Arsenic was available in abundance as a by-product of smelting iron ore. Never before had a would-be murderer access to such easily available toxins. And Agatha exploited that common place availability to the hilt.

Success never went to Agatha's head, however. It couldn't, because she had to fight so many demons in her life, including her childhood poverty and her first husband's infidelity.

She had married the dashing Archie Christie, a member of the Royal Flying Corps, just after the First World War began. Archie later became an inveterate golfer and one day reported that he had fallen in love with Nancy Neele, a good golfer—and that he wanted a divorce.

For months, Agatha tried to reason with him. Then, one night, she drove away. After an hour, she abandoned her car and took a train to Waterloo Station, in London. That same night, she travelled to Harrogate, a spa town in Yorkshire where she checked into the Hydropathic Hotel under the name of Theresa Neele.

The disappearance of the famous mystery author created a national manhunt. More than five hundred policemen tried to comb the downs and drag the ponds in the area around her abandoned car. Over the weekend, hundreds of volunteers, some assisted with bloodhounds, joined in. Major newspapers reported daily on the progress.

Agatha kept on with her shopping, walks, spa visits and even played bridge with some fellow-guests at the hotel. They even discussed the mystery of the missing novelist, but no one could make the connection.

Soon a reward of a hundred pounds came to be announced. Agatha was fond of listening to the hotel's band after dinner.

There in due course the drummer and the saxophonist recognised her. They informed the police, and the world heaved a sigh of relief to find their famous novelist hale and hearty.

In case, the disappearance was Agatha's desperate ploy to regain Archie's affections, it didn't work. They soon divorced and Archie did go ahead and married Neele.

Agatha's family floated the theory that Agatha had suffered an attack of fugue, a form of amnesia. She claimed to remember nothing of what had happened, and her autobiography too utters not a word about the incident.

Agatha's jealous competitors alleged that her contrived disappearance was meant to catch public's attention and to boost sales. If that were so, the strategy was hugely successful. Agatha had produced six murder-mystery novels by that time, and her disappearance, with its interesting link to detective fiction, did turn her in to a celebrity. Publishers immediately ordered reprints of all her earlier novels, which were soon sold out.

A year after her divorce from Archie, Agatha went on a trip to Iraq. There she met an archaeologist, Max Mallowan. They fell in love and soon got married. She was thirty-nine, and Mallowan was twenty-five!

Fortunately, Agatha's second marriage to a younger archaeologist was much more successful. It also rekindled her love for travelling. She could now visit Syria, Lebanon, Egypt, Jordon, and Iraq on so many archaeological expeditions. Her novels could now be set in some very exotic locations.

Everywhere a writing room was erected for her. She also in her spare time volunteered to remove dirt from the relics, using a facial cleanser, and dutifully photographed them.

Agatha travelled often on the Orient Express and this is where her inspiration for the novel *Murder in the Orient Express* came from. Till her last days (she died in 1976, at eighty-five), Agatha remained an inveterate traveller. She visited Greece, Spain, Australia, Canada (she loved Lake Louise), USA (including Hawaii), South Africa, Croatia, Italy, Iran (then called Persia) and her favourite, New Zealand. She often described "travelling as living in a dream."

But the best part was that even after achieving such stupendous success, she remained ever so humble. She was forever reluctant to critique manuscripts of other authors who begged her to do so because she felt that critiquing would discourage budding writers. She believed that all writers have their own unique voice, their own way of expressing things and would have ultimately their own audience.

And in that belief, she served as a beacon of inspiration to million other introvert writers.

Food for thought

Introverts come out better in writing than in speaking. It is no wonder that many writers are introverts themselves.

Now if you are very likely to spend a lot of time in solitude playing with your imagination, then why not write a novel? What has been preventing you from doing so?

Writer's block? Fear of failure? Not enough time?

Why not take inspiration from the untrained and unschooled Agatha Christie then and write novels just to entertain yourself?

"Very few of us are what we seem."

–Agatha Christie

Chapter 2: Wannabe Actor Spends Sleepless Nights on a Public Bench and Becomes a Legend

The year was 1968.

A 26-year old, reasonably well-educated lad, had just chucked away a "regular" well-paying job in Kolkata and moved to Mumbai. Quite like any of those thousand fools who alight every day at the Church Gate station with dreams of making it big in the Indian film industry.

Sure, the young man had acted in some plays in his school and college days. But that was not enough for Mumbai to welcome him with open arms. Everywhere he went, he faced derision and rejection.

One explanation, from those who cared to explain, was that he looked too "unconventional." That is, he did not have that "typical chocolate boy" look that the Indian film industry was looking for its "heroes" in those days.

Another was that at six feet three inches, he was way too tall. Others said he was too dark, too thin and so on.

The young man thought that at least he had a good voice which could be termed as deep, masculine or even baritone. So he applied to the All India Radio, the public broadcaster, and **failed to pass the audition**! He next went to the famous radio presenter Ameen Sayani, and was told on his face that he did not have the "typical" voice required for radio.

The lad came from a decent middle-class family. His father had a doctorate in English literature from Cambridge University. But that didn't help the young man to even find a place to stay in Mumbai. **So he spent many nights sleeping on a public bench on the Mumbai's Marine Drive!**

The young man's parents were quite friendly with the then-Prime Minister of India Mrs. Indira Gandhi. So they got a letter of recommendation sent from her to the famous actor-director Sunil Dutt.

Dutt agreed to cast the young man, but only as a deaf and mute character in his upcoming film "Reshma and Shera." The film was acclaimed as an artistic film but that couldn't stop its sinking on the box office without a trace. In any case, no one could gather how good or bad the young man's voice or dialogue delivery was!

In 1969, when the young man was just about to give up, he got another break. This time it was a low-budget black-and-white film called "Saat Hindustani." Once again, the film flopped but the young man won his first National Award as the best newcomer. Ten more middling films followed. The young man kept on playing bit roles with the super stars of those days like Rajesh Khanna but was still hand-to-mouth.

Then came his 13th movie, in 1973, where he played the role of an honest police officer. The character fought against corruption, not as a police officer on duty, but as an outsider, a vigilante. This was one of the first anti-hero movies in Indian cinema and became a super-hit.

There was no looking back after that.

No longer was the young man being considered for only shy, supporting roles. He was now....THE Angry young man of the Indian film industry. Offers poured in. It was during those days when he met his future wife. As an actor, she looked small and cute to him. She was drawn to his intense eyes and that awesome voice. Both fell in love and got married soon thereafter in 1973.

By 1975, the young man had become a super star, well-known for playing unusual, anti-hero kind of roles. It was said that he channelised all his anger and frustration of his struggling days in portraying authentic, believable characters on screen. He once played the role of a lowly dockyard worker who had no qualms in becoming rich by hook or by crook.

Fans were falling in love with his booming, baritone voice, the same voice which the mandarins of All India Radio had found so unsuited! Eminent directors like Satyajit Ray were hiring him for voice-overs for their films. Every film producer knew that if they cast him, they would have a guaranteed hit on their hands. His fans fought for tickets in the black market at astronomical rates to watch his movies.

And then tragedy struck. The actor was filming a fight scene where the villain gave a perfect shot by hitting the hero hard. Every one clapped in admiration. The actors bowed to thank them all, but something had given way.

At the height of his career, the super star had to be rushed to the intensive care in a hospital. His intestines had ruptured which was a life threatening internal injury. Fans were devastated. Entire India thronged to temples, churches, mosques and gurudwaras to pray for his well-being.

On the operation table, at just 41 years old, the super star died clinically for eleven minutes. But just as it happens in Indian movies, he revived miraculously, with his wife exclaiming, "Look his toe is moving." God had heard the nation's prayers and the legend escaped from the jaws of death.

For almost a decade, the star could not take up any new roles. The 60 bottles of blood that he received during those tense days in the operation theatre transmitted Hepatitis B to him. That destroyed 3/4th of his liver. The unstoppable medical expenses had brought him to the edge of financial bankruptcy.

But the super star fought back. One indication of his grit and determination was that despite his near-fatal accident and subsequent *myasthenia gravis* (a rare muscular disorder), he agreed to perform a stunt from a height of 30 feet for a scene in a Hindi film called *Aks*.

Once again, nothing could stop the super star from reclaiming his position at the summit of the Indian film industry. It was a second life, but that turned him into a living legend.

If you watch Indian movies, I'm sure you would have guessed by now who I'm talking about.

The living legend is: **Amitabh Bachchan.**

Born in 1942, when the Japanese had bombed Pearl Harbour, and the Quit India Movement had just begun in India, Amitabh was born to the eminent Hindi poet Harivansh Rai Bachchan in Allahabad, India. He was first named "Inquilab" representing the poet's deep seated conviction that revolution will one day lead to freedom. His mother Teji Bachchan was a Punjabi, with a passion for theatre. It was no wonder that the boy inherited his artistic legacy from his parents.

Young Amitabh began his studies in Allahabad. He then went to Sherwood College, a boarding school in the hills of

Nainital, where he first discovered his knack and passion for acting. However, as he admits:

"I never thought as a child that I'll enter films. When we went to see films in Allahabad, I never imagined that one day I'll be on the big screen."

Amitabh completed his Masters from Delhi, and soon started looking for a job. But that was not so easy. He faced rejection after rejection.

Amitabh thought there was something wrong with him. May be he was not qualified enough. Or perhaps he was too tongue-tied to express himself well in an interview. Or, or, or....

In sheer desperation, Amitabh moved out of his comfort zone, to a thousand miles eastward, to Kolkata. There he managed his first job with the firm Shaw Wallace. He later joined the shipping firm Bird and Co. as a freight broker.

But something was missing from his life. Amitabh felt empty from within. The job experience was soul-crushing. He was yearning for creative freedom. He had to admit that a "real job" was not for him. His destiny lay somewhere else. Which other profession was right for him?

How about Acting?

Good idea, except that acting in films was considered to be one of the most extroverted professions in the world. And Amitabh was anything but an extrovert.

In one of his interviews, Amitabh admitted that,

"I was very shy as a child. Very shy. Lot of problems with very simple things. Like entering a restaurant all by myself. And even much later when I was looking for work in films, I met Manojji (a famous actor-producer-director) and he said, he was shooting in Filmistan, he said come and see me there. And I used to catch a

train from Churchgate, go to Andheri, walk from the station up to the Filmistan gate. But I just never had the courage to walk in. And I tried to, for seven days, but every time, I came back from the gate. I'm very shy even today. But I must admit that coming into films, and putting myself into situations which are unreal has, perhaps, given me a little more confidence. But initially it was destroying. It destroyed me completely when I went to Hotel Sun 'n' Sand and I saw Manojji doing a song with Sairaji (the popular actress Saira Banu). There were millions of people standing. I was petrified. I remember having sleepless nights. I still do sometimes, when I have to do a song out in the open in front of people. It's not so much the incapability to do the sequence, as the fact that I have to do it when there are millions of eyes watching. I know it's a contradiction to my earlier interest which is theatre. But an introvert, I've always been."

So was Amitabh ashamed of his introvert trait? Not at all. He is grateful for it. He believes he acquired his quiet trait from his father, Mr. Harivansh Rai Bachchan, an eminent poet who wrote a lot of patriotic poems during India's Freedom Struggle.

As he explains:

"My father's more shy. Introvert. But very powerful when it came to his expression, his writing. In many respects you could say that temperamentally I'm like my father. Physically, maybe I have the Sikh blood."

Amitabh Bachchan is a living example of someone who followed his heart, and who never gave up despite all kinds of circumstances, including financial and medical. He will always serve as a beacon of inspiration for millions of quiet artists around the world.

His health parameters continue to deteriorate. His mid-riff area, as he jokes, has become full of holes, because of the probes that doctors have been inserting to treat him. He keeps on going in and out of the operation theatre. He continues to suffer from *myasthenia gravis,* an autoimmune disease that causes muscular weakness and fatigue.

Yet ask him to do a public service broadcast about Polio, or Clean Water, and he is forever willing to do that free of cost. Regardless of the roles that now come his way, he continues to entertain and charm people with his multi-faceted charismatic persona.

Over the years, Amitabh has not only grown bigger and more iconic but he has also become an institution that is inseparable from the lore of Indian cinema.

But beyond that aura, and beyond the facade of the Big B, there beats the soul of a consummate performer—an *artiste* for whom celluloid is simply a dimension of his expression and *raison d'être.*

And the best part is that he is still so humble. Even today, Amitabh loves to point out to that bench every time he drives past it.

"I have never been a superstar and never believed in it."

–Amitabh Bachchan

Some interesting nuggets from Amitabh Bachchan's life:

* Amitabh's first salary in Kolkata was Rupees 500 per month.

* He was paid just Rupees 1,000 for his debut film.

* Amitabh had given 12 consecutive flops before his first big hit Zanjeer.

* His favourite screen name is Vijay as seen in over 20 movies.

* Amitabh Bachchan started being called Big B in late 90's after his second comeback with Mrityudaata.

* During the shooting of Khuda Gawah, a movie set in Afghanistan, the Afghan Government provided Amitabh a cover from the Air Force for his protection. The movie remains the most watched Indian film in the history of Afghanistan.

* The song Rang barse from Silsila and some lyrics from Alaap were penned by his father, Dr. Harvanshrai Bachchan. So is the poetry in Agneepath.

* Amitabh is now a strict vegetarian and a teetotaler.

* Amitabh Bachchan is ambidextrous.

* He is the first Asian actor to have a wax model of his likeness displayed at Madame Tussauds' in London. Another statue was installed in New York and Hong Kong.

* In 2001, Amitabh Bachchan was honoured with the "Actor of the Century" award at an Alexandria Film Festival in Egypt.

* Amitabh was named Actor of the Millennium in a BBC News Poll ahead of such luminaries as Charlie Chaplin, and Marlon Brando.

* In 2003, he was conferred with the honorary citizenship of the French town of Deauville.

* Bruce Willis once commented, at the opening of Planet Hollywood, that Mr. Bachchan was "bigger than any Hollywood star."

* Amitabh was awarded the Padma Bhushan, one of the highest civilian awards in India, in 2001.

* Amitabh hates the word Bollywood, the word that most use to describe the Hindi film industry.

Chapter 3: A Reckless Introvert Becomes "The Most Immaculate Painter" Ever Born

In the beautiful city of Lieden in the Netherlands, there lived a miller named Herman Gerritszoon Van Rijn. Herman was married to Neeltgen Willemsdr Van Zuytbrouck, who was the daughter of a baker.

Lieden was a rich and prosperous town. Two branches of the Old Rhine River, entered the city on the east, and united in the centre of the town. The town was further intersected by numerous small canals lined with trees on both sides.

The couple was blessed with 10 children (with two dying in infancy). On 15 July 1606, their 8th child was born. The boy Van Rijn from his early childhood was different. He was fascinated by nature and the beauty of his picturesque birthplace. He would spend days in solitude admiring the Dutch countryside. The blue sky filled with clouds, the birch, oak, and the maple trees, and the sun sometimes shining bright above the canal or setting above it.

Van Rijn could have become a baker or a miller following family traditions but his parents sent him instead to a Latin school. Everyone in school conversed in Latin and so the boy soon became proficient in Latin. He also received a thorough grounding in history, rhetorical gestures, historical veracity, textual accuracy and classical and biblical stories from the Catholic books of Cicero, Virgil, Caesar, Sallust, Livy, Aesop, etc.

Van Rijn thereafter was admitted to the University of Leiden but couldn't complete his studies. His heart desired something else. His destiny was taking him somewhere else. He wanted to paint. Be an Artist. "He was a master of his own life; lost in the midst of his own small but beautiful world."

Van Rijn's parents were puzzled. But they didn't stand in the way of his artistic inclinations. They sent him to Jacob Van Swavenburgh, an obscure and "not too talented" Leiden painter.

The young man spent the next three years learning the fundamentals of painting from Swavenburgh. Dissatisfied, he moved to Amsterdam to study under Pieter Lastman, known for his historical paintings. During those days, ordinary art buyers used to prefer art depicting scenes of everyday life, landscapes and still life. But Van Rijn was engrossed in painting history and scriptures. He also learnt there the techniques of using light and shade in pictures known as a "Chiaroscuro" device.

At the age of 18 or 19, Van Rijn came back to his father's house in Leiden to practice his craft. He spent days and nights painting all by himself mastering the techniques of etching, an art process where a painter uses glass, copper or a needle to carve on stone. The presence of a master was already reflecting through him.

Within two years, he had established himself as an artist in Leiden. At the age of 21, he started teaching others. "The Stoning of St. Stephen" was one of his earliest paintings, where he in a signature move gave a spectator his own features.

In 1630 his father died which left Van Rijn devastated. The blow was heavy because Herman was an encouraging father and a loving companion to his children. Just around that time, Constantijn Huygens, secretary to Stadholder Frederick Henry, visited the Leiden studio shared by Van Rijn and his friend Jan Lievens. He found them "both brilliant, but too introverted." Soon Huygens could procure the duo important commissions from the Prince of Orange (of the principality of Orange in southern France), who wanted to decorate his under construction Greco-Roman palace with art. As Huygens recorded in his diary, "not even Appelles (one of the very first Greek painters) would have imagined what a young fellow, a Dutchman, the son of a miller, a beardless man, could muster and express."

The prince was overjoyed and soon started paying the two artists the princely sum of six hundred guilders for each painting. But Van Rijn had a mind of his own. He painted the way he wanted to paint and not how others wanted him to paint. He also appeared to be incapable of handling money, and unable to express himself. The Prince found him complicated and very opinionated.

Nonetheless, his reputation of being a remarkable painter of portraits kept on spreading far and wide. The British Ambassador Sir Robert Kerr (1578-1654), later the first Earl of Ancrum, gave several of Van Rijn's paintings to King Charles I. Among them was "his own picture & done by himself."

King Charles I sent an invitation to him to visit England and paint "The Anatomy Lesson of Nicolaes Tulp." In 1632, Van Rijn's completed the painting which was also his first large group portrait. The painting gave him a lot of fame and was a turning point in his career.

Meanwhile his love life too had started blossoming. He fell in love with Saskia Van Uylenburch, the cousin of his landlord and one of the wealthiest women in the Netherlands. She had a pleasant smile and an enchanting personality. Despite being a family of five sisters and three brothers, there appeared to be an empty space within her because of the demise of her parents.

Van Rijn was so smitten with Saskia that he even loaned his landlord Van Uylenburch (and Saskia's cousin and guardian) 1000 florins. This probably ensured that although Van Rijn came from a modest background, Saskia's family members would have no objection to the marriage. Saskia too was willing because Van Rijn by then had established himself as a fabulous painter of the time. They finally got married in 1634.

Saskia was not only the love of Van Rijn's life, but also the inspiration behind many of his paintings. She was "an endearing woman, a statuesque model and an obedient wife." Saskia enhanced his career by bringing him in contact with wealthy patrons who queued up to commission portraits. An exceptionally fine example from this period is said to be the "Portrait of Nicolaes Ruts" (1631, Frick Collection, New York City). In addition, Van Rijn's mythological and religious works were much in demand. He painted numerous dramatic masterpieces such as "The Blinding of Samson" (1636, Frankfurt).

Van Rijn was considered the most fashionable painter of portraits. In a matter of four years, he completed as many as 102 paintings. He got commissions faster than he could paint them. People waited for months to be painted by him. No painter could equal his "chiaroscuro" effects or his style of "bold impasto" (the thick application of a pigment to a canvas in painting).

Soon his studio was filled with pupils, some of whom (such as Carel Fabritius) were already trained artists. Others included: Govert Flinck, Ferdinand Bol, Philips Koninck, Gerbrandt Van Den Eeckhout, Jan Victors, and Leendeert Cornelisz. And in those days, they all were willing to pay as much as 100 florins a year for the privilege to be trained by Van Rijn.

By now, you would have guessed who I am talking about.

Yes, he was indeed **Rembrandt Harmenszoon Van Rijn**.

And he has been declared as the greatest artist of all times along with Shakespeare, Michelangelo, and Raphael.

But life is never a bed of roses. There was a seamier side of Rembrandt's life we can't gloss over.

And that was this one terrible habit he couldn't keep in check—that he spent recklessly. Rembrandt would buy the most expensive pieces of art, jewellery, paintings, and engravings in the name of appreciation of art with no care for his long term financial well-being. During auctions, he would quite stupidly keep bidding higher and higher till he could own whatever he had taken fancy to. Nothing could drill any sense into him and he remained "adamant, strong-willed, recklessly generous, prodigal and carefree."

And then there were personal tragedies after tragedy.

Saskia gave birth to a son who was named Rombertus. Rembrandt was overjoyed. He couldn't resist painting sketches of his newborn son and wife. His happiness, however, was short lived as Rombertus died soon.

A few years later, his wife gave birth to a second child. But once again, tragedy struck and this baby girl, who was named Cornelia, too passed away in just three weeks after her birth. The third child, a daughter (again named Cornelia), died just one month after her birth.

Then Rembrandt's beloved mother passed away. The mother whom he was so connected to. The mother who was the real emotional support of his life. That mother who had such blind belief in his artistic capabilities. That mother for whom he did not want to leave for Amsterdam. Despite the knowledge that in contrast to Leiden, which was a small "university" town, Amsterdam was a city of the "rich" and "wealthy." Full of patrons who could afford lavish portraits of themselves and paintings of historical or religious scenes. His mother's death shattered Rembrandt and almost destroyed him from within.

Meanwhile Saskia gave birth to her fourth child, a son who was named Titus. Happiness seemed to be returning to Rembrandt's family. But alas, that was short lived. Saskia's health had deteriorated. It had become clear she won't survive for long. Probably the birth of four children between 1635 and 1641 was too much of a toll to bear in those days of primitive medical facilities.

Realising that she had little time, Saskia wrote a will on 5th June, 1642 leaving her estate to her husband and her son. Rembrandt could own all the property, principal and interest unless he remarried. In that case, half of the property was to be put in trust for Titus.

Saskia died the same year. She was just 30. Rembrandt was devastated. Everything had gone from his life. The love he craved for, and the financial acumen of Saskia that he needed to support himself.

Rembrandt's career had taken a downturn. He was commissioned to paint "The Night Watch." When the painting was completed, it left people in shock. It wasn't that his art had deteriorated. It was that people found the painting to be too dark and unacceptable to the people who were portrayed in it.

Rembrandt was considered arrogant for not painting them the way they wished to be painted. His paintings ceased to be the attraction of the town. As if this wasn't bad enough, Saskia's relatives began a property dispute with him.

Meanwhile a ray of hope flashed on the horizon. In 1649, seven years after the death of Saskia, Rembrandt fell in love for the second time with Hendrickje Stoffels. She was almost half of Rembrandt's age but had selflessly devoted herself to him as his housekeeper. They couldn't be married because of the conditions stipulated in Saskia's will. This included that Rembrandt had to pay 20,375 florins to Louis Crayers, the guardian of Titus, before he could get married to anybody.

In 1652, Hendrickje gave birth to a child, but the child died soon. In 1654, Hendrickje was blessed with another baby, a daughter who they named Cornelia (again). Rembrandt's family was once again filled with joy at the arrival of an adorable kid.

But Rembrandt's terrible money management was not letting him have an easy time. He was taking loans from all and sundry. His pupils had abandoned him because he was NOT painting as the market wanted. Rembrandt was declared bankrupt in 1656.

Everything he possessed was put out for auction, including his house where he had spent eighteen years of his life. It was an auction not just of his property, but of his reputation, feelings, memories and emotions. All his collection of art and antiquities including, ancient sculptures, Flemish and Italian Renaissance paintings, Far Eastern art, contemporary Dutch works, weapons, and armour, were sold off for ridiculously low amounts.

Even though he couldn't marry Hendrickje due to his financial difficulties, and the clauses in Saskia's will, Rembrandt continued to live with her along with his son Titus and daughter Cornelia. The family moved to a rented house in Rozengracht (now no. 184) in the Jordaan district of Amsterdam. Like Saskia, Hendrickje too became an inspiration for many of his paintings.

Rembrandt continued to paint and produced such great paintings as: The Jewish Bride (1665), The Syndics of the Cloth Guild (1661), Jacob Blessing the Sons of Joseph (1656), and a self-portrait (1658). However, as his eyesight weakened, he couldn't paint the way he used to.

On 15 December 1660, Hendrickje and Titus transferred Rembrandt's company and trade in "paintings, graphic art, engravings and woodcuts" to their names, thus relieving Rembrandt of all financial control. Titus became his universal heir. But tragedies still chased Rembrandt. In 1661 Hendrickje became seriously ill and passed away in 1663.

Rembrandt's son Titus got married to Magdalena Van Loo, daughter of a silversmith (and his cousin) on 28th February, 1668. But the happiness was shockingly short lived. Titus succumbed to plague on 4th September, 1668, when he was just 27. His daughter Titia Van Rijn is recorded to have been baptised in the Nieuwezijds Chapel on 22 March 1669, six months after the death of her father.

Rembrandt was now a heart broken poor old man. The final ray of hope had vanished from his life.

He took his last breath on October 4, 1669, eleven months following the death of his son. He was buried, like any other poor person, in Westerkerk, in Amsterdam, at the foot of a staircase of a church at the cost of thirteen florins.

Rembrandt remained an enigma all his life. Was he a spendthrift or a miser, stubborn or stupid, zealous or reckless—no one label could do justice to his life. But what is established is that Rembrandt had the rare ability to transform the ugliest of face into the most beautiful of paintings.

He once said,

"Of course you will say that I ought to be practical and ought to try and paint the way they want me to paint. Well, I will tell you a secret. I have tried and I have tried very hard, but I can't do it. I just can't do it! And that is why I am just a little crazy."

But thanks to his craziness, we can now experience the "reality" behind numerous human emotions that we probably never could. Today even after four centuries, wherever in the world's topmost museums we come across any work of this genius, we are left simply awestruck.

The late nineteenth-century critic Emile Michel says,

"Rembrandt, in effect, belongs to the race of artists who cannot have descendants, the race of Michelangelo, the race of Shakespeare, of Beethoven; like these Prometheuses of art he wanted to ravish the celestial life, to put the vibrations of life into still form, to express in the visible, that which by its very nature is non-material and indefinable."

Rembrandt museum in Amsterdam today is housed in the same fashionable town house that the great artist had purchased in 1639 when he was 33. The house saw the production of many great paintings alongside many personal tragedies. His first wife and three of his children died there. In 1656 Rembrandt himself, after his bankruptcy, was forced to move out of this house. The new owner was Lieven Simonsz who had bought the property for 11,218 florins. He had then added the upper story and roof, giving it the appearance it today has. The Dutch Government acquired this property in 1911, to honour the memory of this revered national artist and as a good example of 17th Century Dutch architecture.

Food for thought

Rembrandt mastered his techniques in solitude. There is no better way for an introverted artist to improve. If you want to take your craft to the next level, you could do well to spend more time with yourself.

Rembrandt is a terrible example to follow in money management. If you want to be a wealthy artist, therefore, do please ensure that you are financially literate. You should also realise the impact of all your investments and expenses reasonably well.

But as far as your craft goes, do follow Rembrandt in following your heart. Don't worry if your books, paintings, music or films don't do well in the short run. If you keep at it, improving your craft bit by bit, there is no knowing what lady fate may have in store for you.

"A painting by Rembrandt not only stops the time that made the subject flow into the future, but makes it flow back to the remotest ages. By means of this operation Rembrandt achieves solemnity. He thus discovers why, at every moment, every event is solemn: he knows it from his own solitude."

Jean Genet, "Something Which Seemed to Resemble Decay" (1964), trans. Bernard Frechtman, Antaeus (spring 1985 issue)

Chapter 4: A Bored Professor Doodles on a Student's Exam Paper and Creates a Global Blockbuster

John would walk down the road, lost in his thoughts, with a befuddled smile occasionally creasing his face. His hair greying, his visage calm but wrinkled with his myriad worldly-wise experiences. Some people passed by, without really noticing him.

John would involuntarily take a sigh of relief. He hated being treated like a celebrity. Letters from fans pouring into his mailbox by the thousands would annoy him no end. His phone's constant ringing would drive him crazy. People wanted to know more about his unique characters. They wanted to understand and even use the strange language he had created.

John, like all introverts, abhorred being in the public eye. He wanted a life where he could quietly focus on his creative pursuits. That is why he admired Oxford, with its dreamy spires and lolling green meadows, so much. It was not that he was unsocial. But he preferred spending more time with his family or friends than with his fans.

He did occasionally go to parties, sometimes even dressed as a polar bear. This was probably to prove the point that he was not a typical stuck up, reserved, and aloof Oxford don. But he still liked maintaining a low profile. And there was no other place quieter than Oxford to do so. The place really suited his personality.

His spreading fame would often startle him. He didn't know when and how his tales of mighty kings, glorious citadels, massive armies, and great battles had become the latest craze in Britain. Fans devoured it and asked for more. Critics either praised it or panned it as the worst piece of literature ever published in the history of mankind.

"He is more of a Story Teller than an author," some whined.

John was angry to learn that his books had been pirated and were being sold in millions in the United States. He wanted to upbraid his publishers for being so slow in crossing the Atlantic. At the same time, he felt secretly flattered that someone had taken the trouble to pirate his books.

This new series had become the bible of the "Alternative Society" and had started a fantasy revolution. First, Dungeons and Dragons, a role playing game, was created and soon became all the rage in the late sixties and early seventies. Then it was alleged (and even confirmed by George Lucas) that the famous "Star Wars" series in Hollywood was inspired by John's trilogy.

Everyone wanted to know what he was writing next. Journalists wanted to interview him. But like all quiet people, John hated all this intrusiveness. So he just moved away to Bournemouth to finish another volume. Meanwhile magazines complained that it was easier to get an interview with the British Prime Minister than with John!

Who was this John? Let's start at the beginning.

John was born in 1892 in Bloemfontein in South Africa. His life was full of strange happenings, including his "stealing" by his family's trusted servant Isaak who brought him to his village to show how a white baby looked!

Later, once wandering out in his garden, John noticed a large black object that looked like a glove. He moved forwards to check out and tripped and fell on it. The black thing suddenly came alive and bit him.

John got up and ran across the garden crying out in pain till his nanny stopped him and noticed the insect bite on his hand. She recognised that it was the bite of a dangerous Tarantula. Reacting instinctively, as she was trained to do in the bush, the nanny put her mouth to the site of the bite and sucked out the poison. John survived, but the incident haunted him for the rest of his life. Spiders appeared in his stories off and on as those creepy, crawly, twisted, evil things.

Unfortunately, John lost his father when he was just four. Then he lost his mother, of all things to Diabetes, when he was twelve. John's grandparents had already disowned John's mother because she along with her children had converted to Catholicism. So John along with his brother had to be moved to a boarding home where a Catholic priest took care of them. It was there that he first met Edith Bratt.

John soon fell in love with that beautiful girl. But there was a technical hitch. Edith was three years older to John. When the priest discovered, about what he thought was an infatuation not in accordance with the mores of those days, he moved Edith away.

John was, however, undeterred and the moment he could stand on his feet, away from those boarding homes, he married Edith on March 22, 1916 in Warwick.

John had gone to Oxford to study classics, Old English, Gothic, Welsh and Finnish. The course did not challenge or titillate his intellect one bit. So he received a disappointing low second class.

John then decided to switch over to English Language and Literature. His hard work and determination paid off when he achieved a first-class degree at Exeter College in Honour Moderations.

In 1916 World War I was looming on the horizon. John believed that what Germany did was pure evil. He enlisted himself with the Lancashire Fusiliers as a Second Lieutenant. He kissed Edith good bye and went to train at Staffordshire. John finally saw action in the battle of Somme.

The battle was hailed as a victory, but not for John. He had lost most of his closest friends. John had survived the war, but his soul was scarred forever. He was haunted by fearful thoughts, flashbacks and bad dreams. The war had left him emotionally empty and numb. In medical terms, he was suffering from PTSD or Post-Traumatic Stress Disorder.

Intermittently he also suffered from Trench Fever, an infectious disease characterised by fever, headache, sore muscles, bones, and joints, and skin lesions. Apparently body lice, from the unwashed soldiers who fought in the trenches, used to transmit this disease. The illness was serious enough to warrant John's hospitalisation for a month in Birmingham.

To sort out the strange mess of feelings, John plunged into writing. Themes of gnomes and elves, the rise and fall of the gods and their children, and a brooding evil became central to his stories. In 1925, he got an offer to teach at Oxford. At this time, John had also become interested in the origins of the Welsh language. He was the founding member of a club of writers called *The Inklings*, which counted among its members C.S. Lewis and Owen Barfield. They met often over a drink to discuss literary works. Once again, John had created a new group of friends with whom he could share his interests and passion.

One day, John was busy correcting exam papers, a hopelessly dull job that could bore any professor to death. He discovered a page left blank accidentally by the examinee. John's wild imagination took over. Did a wizard cast a spell on this page? Or whether an unnatural dark force had taken control of the student?

Suddenly John overcame with an uncontrollable urge to write something on that blank piece of paper. As if he was possessed, he took out his pen and scribbled:

"In a hole in the ground there lived a Hobbit."

Mind you, not rabbit, but HOBBIT. But what does a hobbit mean? Now John had to figure that out!

So he wrote short stories describing these little human-like creatures with hair on their feet. These stories were later discovered by Susan Dagnall, an employee of the publishing firm George Allen and Unwin. She asked John to tell her more about these interesting characters. So he wrote whatever he knew about Hobbits and sent a compilation of short stories to her. These were then presented to the Chairman who gave these to his 10-year old son to read. The son loved it and the book was published in 1937 as "*The Hobbit.*"

The book became wildly successful among both children and adults. So the Chairman asked John whether he had any other work on similar lines. John presented the Chairman with a compilation of short stories and poems which he called "*Quenta Silmarillion.*"

The Chairman's reaction was mixed. He liked John's writing but didn't care much for his poetry. *The Silmarillion*, therefore, was not published. John was devastated. He had spent nearly 20 years compiling this tome. However, he agreed to write a sequel to "*The Hobbit.*"

It took him 16 years more of hard work to finish the massive project. He poured all his wisdom and imagination in these stories. He spent hundreds of hours punching away on his typewriter. What he finished was a work that touched the heart of millions.

The book was known by the popular name of "**The Lord of the Rings.**" Inspired by ancient European myths, with its own sets of maps, lore and languages, it was a compilation of six books squeezed into three volumes.

John released part one of the series, *The Fellowship of the Ring*, in 1954. *The Two Towers* and *The Return of the King* followed in 1955, finishing up the trilogy. The books gave readers a rich literary trove populated by elves, goblins, talking trees and all manner of fantastic creatures, including characters like the wizard Gandalf and the dwarf Gimli.

BBC put a condensed version of the series on its radio station in 12 segments in 1956. Money was just pouring in thereafter.

You would have guessed by now who this John was. His friends referred to him as Tollers. His full name was John Ronald Reuel Tolkien or **J.R.R. Tolkien**. Some of his fans also called him J.R.R.T. which he didn't seem to mind.

Undoubtedly Tolkien had a very high IQ. This was proved by his rapid ascent to academic eminence (Professorship at 32), and his general ability to understand and learn rapidly. He was also known for his ability to solve novel problems, and to reason abstractly.

Living at an extraordinarily vivid and creative time, Tolkien has been hailed as a creative genius, even as an "Author of the Century." The world he created in his fantasy trilogy was totally a figment of his imagination, yet so engrossing that anyone could relate to it.

Tolkien retired from Oxford in 1959 and moved to Bournemouth. But his creative juices were still flowing. He soon published an essay and poetry collection, *Tree and Leaf*, and the fantasy tale *Smith of Wootton Major*.

John's wife Edith died in 1971. Overwhelmed by the loss, John put aside *The Silmarillion* and moved back to Oxford with rooms provided by Merton College. In 1973, at 81, Tolkein received from the British Queen the *Order of the British Empire*. Sadly, he also died the same year on September 2, 1973. He was survived by four children.

Tolkien's son Christopher took over the mantle of editing several works that weren't completed at the time of his father's death. This included *The Silmarillion* and *The Children of Húrin*, which were published posthumously. *The Art of the Hobbit* was published in 2012 and contained Tolkien's original illustrations.

Food for thought

J.R.R. Tolkien failed miserably whenever he set out to do things he was not passionate about. But when his passion and creativity combined, amazing things happened. This is evident from his whole life.

Tolkein got poor grades when he was studying Classics. When he switched to English, he started excelling, receiving scholarships and a full Oxford Professorship at the age of 32. Earlier, in his quest to be in Oxford, he had agreed to work as an Assistant Lexicographer on the Oxford English Dictionary. But that career was short-lived as Tolkein hated working on dictionaries. Many of his manuscripts remained unfinished and abandoned years later because they were around topics that he was not really fond of.

But when he cared about things, magic happened. His "Lord of the Rings" fantasy trilogy series has become immortal. The Rings trilogy was also adapted by director Peter Jackson into a highly popular, award-winning trio of films starring Ian McKellen, Elijah Wood, Cate Blanchett and Viggo Mortensen, among others.

Instead of being a "rather typically stuffy and inhibited English Professor of his stuffy and inhibited era," John was perceived as extremely quick-witted. On the whole, JRR Tolkien was an extraordinary man, with an extraordinary mind, who was not just intellectually brilliant but also wildly creative.

Many writers have since tried to create stories hoping to rival "The Lord of the Rings" but have failed miserably. J.R.R. Tolkien had a unique vision, voice and a perspective that no one could come close to.

The big question is: What are you passionate about? Introverts speak less but are often gifted with a rich imagination. Have you ever thought of combining your passion with your creative imagination?

Take inspiration from J.R. R. Tolkien and do what you love doing.

"All that is gold does not glitter,
Not all those who wander are lost;
The old that is strong does not wither,
Deep roots are not reached by the frost.
From the ashes a fire shall be woken,
A light from the shadows shall spring;
Renewed shall be blade that was broken,
The crownless again shall be king."
–J.R.R. Tolkien, The Fellowship of the Ring

Chapter 5: The Quiet Mozart of Madras

In a small school in Madras (now called Chennai), in India, there was a boy named Dileep. His hair was unruly and so long that it kept falling over his eyes.

"Dileep, get your hair cut," ordered his teachers but to no avail. Ever so absent-minded, the boy continued to wear his hair long.

His teachers called him painfully shy. He tried to always sit in the front row, but kept his head down as if in deep contemplation. And he would just not speak, or smile!

As much as he hated attracting any attention, Dileep was nonetheless in great demand. And this was because of his uncanny mastery over musical notes.

He had learnt to play the piano when he was just four. Dileep had obviously inherited his musical genes from his father, who used to compose and write songs for films in the South Indian languages, viz. Tamil and Malayalam.

The school used to organise cultural programmes occasionally. Dileep was the only one who could play the keyboards brilliantly—and the only one who could compose. So willy-nilly, Dileep was thrust into the limelight.

But exasperatingly, Dileep would never follow instructions. During musical concerts, his teachers would ask him to look up and look the crowd in the eye but he would never comply. He would just listen to his heart and play as he wished. When others asked him to "play happy music," he would play "sad music," if that was what his heart desired!

If anyone told the teachers that one day this absent-minded student would be a world class music director winning Grammies and composing for Bollywood, Hollywood and Broadway blockbusters, they would have fainted!

However, Dileep continued to have a difficult childhood. He lost his father when he was just 9. His family had suddenly no regular source of income. To survive, they had to rent out his father's musical instruments.

Dileep soon dropped out of school. He had a mother and three sisters to care for. So by the age of 11, he was playing piano professionally to earn a living.

His talents didn't go unnoticed. Soon he was playing along with such world class artists like Zakir Hussain (the Tabla maestro) and L. Shankar (the violinist). Even in his teens, Dileep was accompanying such greats on their world tours.

Dileep's hard work paid off when he won a scholarship to study Western Classical Music at Trinity College, Oxford. The journey was, however, not easy. Dileep had to master a foreign musical heritage in a foreign language in a foreign setting. But he did all that with aplomb.

Back in India, work initially came through jingles for TV and radio. Dileep grabbed the opportunity with both his hands and went on to compose music for more than 300 jingles. The experience taught Dileep the discipline to convey a powerful message or mood in a very short time.

The quiet person that Dileep was, he deployed most of his earnings to set up a world-class studio in his own house. This enabled him to compose music at home, in splendid solitude, and often in the dead of the night!

It was during those days in the early 1990s when he chanced to meet the famous film director Mani Ratnam. Mani had heard a few samples of Dileep's work and was so impressed that he signed him for his forthcoming Tamil film *Roja*. The music album was a roaring hit even among non-Tamil audience. Offers started pouring in and there was no stopping what Dileep could do with his music.

Dileep's first contract for a Hindi movie album was for the film *Rangeela* in 1995. The massive success of its unusual tunes led him to compose many more hit albums. His subsequent performances in *Bombay* (1995), *Dil Se*, *Taal* (1999), *Zubeida* (2001), *Lagaan* (2001), *Rockstar* (2011), *Jab Tak Hai Jaan* (2012), *Tamasha* (2016) and so on were simply out of this world. Dileep could compose music for over 100 movies in both Bollywood and Hollywood. His albums have sold more than 100 million copies all over the world.

Dileep's biggest success came in 2008 when he became the first Asian to win a Golden Globe Award, a British Academy of Film and Television Arts (BAFTA) Award, and two Academy awards for the songs "Jai Ho" and "O Saya" from the film *Slumdog Millionaire*. His Hollywood movie "Couples Retreat" won him the BMI London Award for Best Score. Ron Fair, a composer and a songwriter from LA declared him to be "one of the world's greatest living composers in any medium."

You would have guessed by now who I'm referring to.

The genius goes by the name of Allah Rakha Rahman, or **A. R. Rahman.**

N.B. Dileep's name was changed by his mother. Distraught by her husband's death, and the consequent misfortune that befell her family, she had visited a Sufi Saint's *dargah* (shrine). There she was advised to embrace Islam and change her son's name to A. R. Rahman, which she did.

Rahman has an amazing ability to straddle different musical traditions: Western, Eastern or Indian. His compositions have integrated styles from jazz to rock, pop to West-end, religious traditions such as Bhajans and Sufi Music, and even themes from West Asian cultures.

A two-time winner and a five-time nominee in the Oscars, Rahman has performed for audiences all over the world. He has also composed music for Chinese films such as "*Warriors of Heaven and Earth*" in 2003.

Rahman's story is truly a rags to riches story. He is also an inspiration to millions of quiet artists from all around the world. Deeply spiritual and ever so humble, he hasn't led his success fuel his ego. He still remembers the day when he had come back home, depressed and disillusioned with life. Sensing his mood, his mother had advised, "Why don't you live for others and then you will find a meaning to life."

After winning the Oscars, Rahman was asked, "What's left for you to achieve?"

He replied: "*Well, I have not achieved anything. I have not ended poverty. I have not stopped wars from happening........I am just a small musician who has got an award and that is it!*"

So what could quiet artists really learn from him?

Never leave home, if that's what pleases you.

Mumbai is considered a mecca for Indian artists, a city where so many dreams have been fulfilled. It would have been easier for Rahman to make a living settled in Mumbai. But instead he chose to stay at home. In Chennai, where he created a world class studio called "Panchathan Record Inn" in his backyard. This is today one of India's most well-equipped and advanced sound recording studios.

Rahman even today creates music from there. While he is at home and comfortable. What people don't know or often ignore is—he has had major success only working from home. It is only here where he can give his 100% time and commitment to nurture his creative forces.

Today Rahman continues to soar to ever greater heights with his musical compositions. Watching his progress, we can be inspired by the way he has turned his introversion in to his strength, confounding critics. Satyajit Bhatkal in his book, "The Spirit of Lagaan," accuses Rahman of being "*a recluse, an introvert to the point of being afraid of any public interface.*"

Bhatkal says, "*his (Rahman's) work as a composer takes place through the dead of the night, in his studio lit by the candles of a holy dargah. Silence and loneliness are his constant companions at work. Perhaps, it is only the inspiration that comes from such a spiritual journey that could have produced the music he has. Were Rahman sensitive to the tensions of the producers, could he ever have been creatively as fertile!*"

But this is what an unapologetic A.R. Rahman said about solitude:

"Your inner voice is the voice of divinity. To hear it, we need to be in solitude, even in crowded places."

Despite being committed to excellence, Rahman remains an intense family man. He adores his mother and dotes on his wife Saira Banu and the children, Rahima, Ameena and Khatija.

He also loves his home and neighbourhood in Chennai. The night he returned to India after receiving the OSCARS, he appealed that his fans don't visit his locality disturbing his neighbours. That was some consideration!

Rahman also boldly draws a line between being religious and being spiritual. He declares that, "*Religion sounds vulgar these days, I am more of a spiritual person. And I believe in being consistent with my spirituality............ It is the most beautiful passion. It raises you above all the negativities. For me and my music, spirituality is the most important element and I don't think I can create the kind of music I do, if I don't practice spirituality.*"

Critics try to tear him apart. They call him names. Some claim that people who like his music must have a very poor taste. Rahman doesn't react. He lets his fans decide, what is great and what is not. He lets his work speak for itself.

"I divide criticism into two categories— one coming from those who understand music, who are worthy of being critical because they are knowledgeable about what they are saying; and then there is another category of people who would criticise you anyway, whether your work is good or bad."

–A. R. Rahman

Chapter 6: A Much-bullied Boy Fails to Get Admission in a Film School and Becomes the Highest Earning Movie Director in History

The quiet dreamy boy came back from school with a bloody nose, AGAIN. He had obviously been bullied. He was smacked and kicked around. What was really the matter?

That his classmates thought he was an idiot?

That his teachers called him lazy?

That he was different?

The problem was—nobody thought he had a problem.

The boy, let's call him Steve, was just so exasperating!

He would fail to complete his homework, without fail. He showed no inclination to enhance his ability to read or write. Steve had to be then labelled a poor, indisciplined, and insolent student who had to be taught a lesson in his own interest.

To compound the problems, Steve day dreamed a lot, in a rather determined manner. He also took every shove and snigger in his stride.

"*I never felt like a victim*," Steve said once.

Heart of heart, Steve suspected that he had a learning disability, but he never made that an excuse.

Like all day-dreamers, he had other things on his mind.

Movies were one.

Steve loved films. Worse, he wanted to make films.

Steve believed that movies could transform a person's life. He thought they could uplift people and save them from feeling shame.

He thought it'd be great if he could make movies not for money but because they needed to be made. He thought it to be a good idea if he could explore unpopular topics like slavery, war, terrorism and the holocaust.

It appears that God heard this boy's unconventional prayers.

Steve grew up and went on to make countless blockbusters. Thanks to his will-power and an immense belief in himself, Steve is today so famous, that his security thinks he would get mobbed, if he steps out unescorted, anywhere in the world.

So who is this person really and what is his story?

Steve was born in an Orthodox Jewish family on December 18, 1946 in Cincinnati, Ohio, U.S. His grandparents, from his father's side, used to live in an area of Austria which is now a part of Poland. His ancestors from his mother's side came from Odessa in Ukraine. In USA, his mother owned a restaurant and his father was an electrical engineer involved in the development of computers.

At 12, Steve made his first 8 mm film "The Last Gunfight" which was about nine minutes long. In a magazine interview he said—this all happened rather accidentally. He had to do a photography assignment, and he found his dad's still camera broken. So he asked the scoutmaster if he could use his dad's movie camera instead. And that was how the movie bug bit him.

A year later, Steve won a prize for a 40 minute war film "Escape to Nowhere." The film's cast composed of his high school friends. People agreed that the boy obviously had a knack for film making.

Steve went on to make 15 more amateur 8mm films. At sixteen, he wrote and directed his first independent film, a 140-minute science fiction adventure called "Firelight." The film was shown in a local cinema for just one evening, but it recouped its cost of $500!

Encouraged, and after finishing his school, Steve applied for admission to the University of Southern California's film school. He was rejected because he had an average Grade "C."

Then a miracle happened.

Steve got a small unpaid internship with Universal Studios where he had to write and direct a short film. Steve jumped at the opportunity, abandoned his academic career and made a gripping short film.

The Universal Studios' Vice President Sidney Sheinberg was so impressed that he offered Steve a seven year directing contract right away. That made Steve the youngest director ever to sign such a long-term deal with Hollywood. His next film on the horror unleashed by a man-eating shark was the highest-grossing film of its time.

Steve ate, drank and breathed only movies. He directed these to escape the mundane realities, and to express his own pain and suffering. He was haunted by his parents' divorce. He was disturbed with the accounts of how Jews had suffered in Nazi Germany. He couldn't see any glory in wars. He used all these emotions to craft movies.

Steve even used his inability to connect with his peers at school to create a movie, where a boy makes friends with an extra-terrestrial creature. The movie was a major blockbuster.

Steve had directed movies that defined the genre they were made in. Any movie buff or film critic worth his salt had to study compulsorily Steve's craft of making movies. The list was long and included E.T., Indiana Jones, Jurassic Park, Amistad, Saving Private Ryan, Catch Me If You Can, Minority Report and the Schindler's List.

So who is this Steve?

Yes, he is the one and only **Steven Allan Spielberg**.

There is no doubt that Spielberg is the most successful movie director in the history of mankind. And yes, he did suffer from Dyslexia, which is a condition in which the brain fails to recognise symbols the way most others do. This then severely decreases a person's accuracy while reading, writing and spelling. As Steven admitted, he took more than two years to learn how to read.

Sadly, Steven's dyslexia wasn't considered a disability throughout his childhood. In fact it was diagnosed only when he was sixty years old! Yet, Spielberg never made his dyslexia as an excuse for defeat. In fact, he happily took part in a video interview explaining how he "dealt with it by making movies."

"*Movies really helped me, kind of saved me from shame, from guilt, from putting it on myself ... when it wasn't my burden...... I think making movies was my great escape, it was how I could get away from all that,"* admits Steven.

Spielberg even used his experiences in school to produce and co-write a movie titled "The Goonies." The film, an "80s cult classic," depicted a "quirky click of friends" who, like Steven, couldn't quite come up to the usual expectations of playing sports like other students.

Spielberg thought ET was the most personal movie he had ever made. He used to find his parents' constant bickering traumatic. He said he would stuff towels under the door to shut out the noise of their fights. As he explained,

"ET is less about a cute extra-terrestrial coming to Earth, more about the nature of divorce in America. In the film, the boy's parents are divorced and his father is always away from home. ET is his way of filling the void."

This tension in parent-child relationships persisted in many of Spielberg's films. Fathers were often found to be missing, reluctant or ignorant. In "Hook," Peter Banning starts off as a reluctant married-to-his-work father who over time regains the respect of his children. In "Indiana Jones and the Last Crusade," Indy's father, who is a professor of medieval literature, seems more interested in his studies of the Holy Grail, than in his own son. In "Schindler's List," Oskar Schindler is reluctant to have a child with his wife. "Munich" has Avner as a man away from his wife and newborn daughter. In "Catch Me If You Can," Frank Abagnale's mother and father part ways quite early in the film.

Steven thinks that "*children from a divorced home are always damaged.*"

The damage in his case appears to have led to a whole lot of neuroses—from nail-biting to phobias about flying, the seas, insects, darkness, lifts, even of furniture with feet!

"*I'm still afraid of lifts,*" admits this celebrated director sheepishly. "*It's a run around sometimes. I have to go through so much hassle to take the stairs. I have to get people to unlock stairwells. Especially in Paris, where the lifts are so small. I walk ten floors to avoid them.*"

While growing up in an affluent white neighbourhood of Cincinnati, Steven encountered a lot of anti-Semitism. Once some school-kids gathered outside his family home chanting, "The Spielbergs are dirty Jews." Classmates would cough the word Jew into their hands when they passed by him.

Steven's father, Arnold Spielberg, always had to move house because of his work— from Ohio to New Jersey, then to Phoenix, Arizona and to finally Saratoga, in northern California. But wherever the family went they faced anti-Semitism. There was a point when after hearing regular anti-Jew remarks about the size of his nose, Steven attempted to stop it growing downward by tying it with tape!

As Steven now reflects,

"The nature of the anti-Semitism was always lack of education. Not understanding what a Jew is. Anti-Semites invest a lot of ethnic, cultural stereotype and evil to something that scares them....... The effect it had on me was to turn me into a loner. It made me withdrawn and self-conscious and even turned me away from my family, who I was angry at for making me a Jew... I think I would have been a social reject anyway, even if I had been Protestant or Lutheran or Episcopalian. I would still have been introverted."

At a personal level, however, Spielberg knew how twenty members of his family were murdered in the Nazi concentration camps. He felt driven, therefore, to give an account of the Holocaust without trivialising that mindboggling tragedy.

As he explains,

"It did take me ten years to start work on Schindler's List and part of that was due to my fear that I wasn't going to be able to acquit myself in a manner that would bring anything less than

shame to the memory of the Holocaust. I didn't want to belittle or trivialise it. I worked hard not to soften it or make it easy to watch. The film doesn't have a positive ending. You know the victims will be ravaged with nightmares for the rest of their lives."

Richard Dreyfuss, star of "Jaws" and "Close Encounters of the Third Kind," once described Steven as a kid of 12 who decided to make movies—and is still 12. Spielberg agrees that he didn't really mature as a film-maker until he made Schindler's List.

Steven is, of course, a self-confessed introvert. He still can't get himself to read reviews of his work and doesn't seem to care about what critics say of him.

He still has a "shaky stomach" before he goes to parties, even with a close group of friends. He is always tongue tied for the first ten minutes not knowing how to start a conversation, a feeling which is so familiar to introverts.

"*Two people standing there who don't know what to say to each other. That happens a lot*," admits Spielberg.

Awards and accolades follow Spielberg wherever he goes. He won the Academy Award for Best Director twice: for "Schindler's List" (1993) and "Saving Private Ryan" (1998). "Schindler's List" also won the Oscar for Best Picture. "Jaws" had earlier won three Academy Awards (for editing, original score and sound). "Close Encounters of the Third Kind" (1977) won Oscars in two categories (Cinematography) and a Special Achievement Award for Sound Effects Editing. "The Adventures of Tintin" won the award for Best Animated Feature Film at the Golden Globe Awards in 2011.

In 1998 Steven was honoured with the Federal Cross of Merit with Ribbon of the Federal Republic of Germany. In 1999 he received the US Department of Defense Medal for Distinguished Public Service. In 2001, Queen Elizabeth II honoured him as a Knight Commander of the Order of the British Empire (KBE). In 2004, Spielberg was admitted as knight of the Légion d'honneur by the then-French President Jacques Chirac. In 2011, he was honoured as a Commander of the Belgian Order of the Crown. In 2015, he was awarded the Presidential Medal of Freedom from President Barack Obama.

In 2006, Premiere listed him as the most powerful and influential figure in the motion picture industry. Time included him in the list of the 100 Most Important People of the Century. In 2009, Boston University presented him an honorary Doctor of Humane Letters degree. Steven was selected as the President of the jury for the 2013 Cannes Film Festival. Forbes' list of the Most Influential Celebrities in 2014 listed Spielberg as the most influential celebrity in America. Jess Cagle, the managing editor of Entertainment Weekly, called Spielberg "*... arguably (well, who would argue?) the greatest filmmaker in history.*"

While not caring for monetary rewards, three of Steven's films—"Jaws" (1975), "E.T. the Extra-Terrestrial" (1982), and "Jurassic Park" (1993)—beat all box office records. With box office collections exceeding $9 billion worldwide, Spielberg is easily the highest-grossing director in history. His personal net worth could be over $3 billion.

Like most introverts, Spielberg likes familiarity and prefers working with the same production members in films after films. For example, Kathleen Kennedy has served as producer on almost all his major films from "E.T." onwards. Similarly, for cinematography, Steven's childhood friend Allen Daviau has shot from the early Spielberg film "Amblin" to "Empire of the

Sun." Again film editor Michael Kahn has edited every film directed by Spielberg from "Close Encounters" to "Munich" (except "E.T."). And for music, Spielberg has worked with John Williams for almost all his films (except three) since "The Sugarland Express."

Despite being super-successful, Steven is extremely modest and simple. He prefers roaming around in his favourite pair of jeans. He was once mistaken for a fixer of a Coke machine by a journalist!

It is humbling to find such a great creative genius coming across as a bit defensive with hunched shoulders and hands clasped between knees. But Spielberg takes pride in being ordinary and anonymous. He loves the simplicity of life: getting up at six a.m., making breakfast for the family, dropping his seven children (including two adopted) to school and so on.

For him, life is not worth living if you can't do a car pool.

"You shouldn't dream your film, you should make it!"

–Steven Spielberg

Chapter 7: The Quiet "Godly Teacher" Who Wrote National Songs of Three Countries and Became the First Non-European Nobel Laureate in Literature

He wrote his first poetry at the age of 8!

He never went to school.

He composed over 2200 songs.

His stories and novels have inspired more than 20 movies from 1927 to 2012.

He was a poet, a novelist, a music composer, a painter, a playwright, and an inveterate traveller who covered more than thirty countries on five continents.

Critics accused him of being too self-obsessed and introverted while others called him a quiet genius, an intellectual rock star.

He influenced such figures as the Japanese Nobel laureate Yasunari Kawabata, Chileans Pablo Neruda and Gabriela Mistral; Mexican writer Octavio Paz; and Spaniards José Ortega y Gasset, Zenobia Camprubí, and Juan Ramón Jiménez.

His works were translated into English, Dutch, German, Spanish, and other languages by eminent persons such as: the British poet Yeats, Czech Indologist Vincenc Lesný, French

Nobel Laureate André Gide, Russian poet Anna Akhmatova, and the former Turkish Prime Minister Bülent Ecevit.

His poetry was set to music for soprano and string quartet by composer Arthur Shepherd.

Alexander Zemlinsky's "Lyric Symphony," Josef Bohuslav Foerster's "cycle of love" songs, Leoš Janáček's famous chorus "Potulný šílenec" ("The Wandering Madman") were all based on his songs.

His lyrics inspired Garry Schyman's "Praan," which accompanied Internet celebrity Matt Harding's 2008 viral video.

Anglo-Dutch composer Richard Hageman translated and set to music his poetry to produce a highly regarded art song: "Do Not Go, My Love."

The second movement of Jonathan Harvey's "One Evening" (1994) was from one of his letters, as was Harvey's earlier piece "Song Offerings" (1985).

He established a new university based on the ancient Indian tradition of *ashramas* where gurus and disciples lived together in the middle of a forest.

He was the first non-European to receive a Nobel Prize for Literature in 1913.

He was granted Knighthood in 1915 which he returned in 1919 after the ghastly Jallianwalla Bagh massacre in Punjab.

He was the voice of the Indian National Movement and had the stature to criticise even Mahatma Gandhi.

He is famous for his song "Ekla Chalo Re" or literally "If They Answer Not to Thy Call, Walk Alone My friend...." in English.

India, Bangladesh, and Sri Lanka have honoured him by making three of his songs as their National Anthems.

You would have guessed the name of this legendary artist by now.

Yes, he is....

Rabindranath Tagore.

Bengalis pronounced his name as *Robindronath Thakur*. His compatriots called him *Gurudev* (the godly teacher). But everyone agreed that he was a polymath who reshaped Bengali literature, music and Indian art (with Contextual Modernism) in the late 19th and early 20th centuries.

Born in the Jorasanko mansion in Calcutta on 7 May 1861, Tagore was the youngest of the thirteen surviving children of parents Debendranath Tagore (1817–1905) and Sarada Devi (1830–1875). Debendranath was a leader of the Brahmo Samaj. This was a new religious sect in the nineteenth-century Bengal which was attempting to revive Hinduism on the basis of ancient texts as *Upanishads*.

Tagore family was very active supporting literary magazines, theatre and recitals of Bengali and Western classical music. Tagore's eldest brother Dwijendranath was a philosopher and poet. Another brother, Satyendranath, was the first Indian to get into the elite and fiercely competitive Indian Civil Service. Jyotirindranath, another brother, was a musician, composer, and playwright. Sister Swarnakumari was a novelist.

Tagore wrote his first poetry as an eight-year-old. He completed a set of major works by 1877 when he was just 16. One of them was a long poem in the old *Maithili* style of poet *Vidyapati*. As a prank, he claimed that these were the lost works of a "newly discovered 17th century *Vaiṣhṇava* poet *Bhānusiṃha*." Funnily, experts gladly accepted the claim!

At sixteen, Tagore directed his brother Jyotirindranath's adaptation of *Molière's Le Bourgeois Gentilhomme*. At twenty, he wrote his first drama-opera: *Valmiki Pratibha* (The Genius of Valmiki).

His play Dak Ghar (The Post Office, 1912) gleaned rave reviews in Europe. It was hailed as a story with borderless appeal. One reason was that it dealt with death as "spiritual freedom" from "the world of hoarded wealth and certified creeds."

This "strange" philosophy had a profound effect on the Jews stuck in Hitler's infamous concentration camps. In July 1942, in the Nazi-overrun Warsaw Ghetto, orphans in the care of Polish doctor-educator Janusz Korczak staged this play in Polish. Biographer Betty Jean Lifton suspected that Korczak did this to prepare the children into accepting death, which looked inevitable.

Tagore hated formal education. Instead, he preferred to roam the family estates or the nearby Bolpur and Panihati idylls. His sojourn at the famous Presidency College of Kolkata lasted just one day. Years later he held that proper teaching should not explain things, but just stoke curiosity. He depicted beautifully his hatred for rote learning in "The Parrot's Training," in which a caged bird is force-fed textbook pages—to death.

Tagore's father wanted him to become a barrister, just as so many prominent Indians like Mahatma Gandhi or Moti Lal Nehru were. So at 17, in 1878, Tagore was sent to England to study at a public school in Brighton, East Sussex. He stayed in a house, that the Tagore family owned named Medina Villas, near Brighton and Hove.

He then enrolled at University College London to study Law, but soon dropped out. Instead he kept on studying

Shakespeare, and other English litterateurs on his own. In 1880, he returned home with no degree.

In 1883, he married Mrinalini Devi. They had five children, two of whom died in childhood. In 1890, he began managing the Tagore family's vast ancestral estates in Shelaidaha (now in Bangladesh). This brought him closer to poor people and increased his interest in social reforms.

As a landlord or "*Zamindar Babu*" as he was called, Tagore travelled across his marshy and riverine holdings in *Padma*, his luxurious family barge. He would collect mostly token rent of rice and get down to share a meal with villagers. During one of such visits, Tagore met Gagan Harkara, who introduced him to the folk songs of Baul Lalon Shah.

Tagore went all out to popularise Lalon's songs. Also from 1891–1895, he wrote his three-volume, 84-story compilation called *Galpaguchchha* (a bouquet of stories). Many of these "ironic and grave tales" focussed on the endemic poverty of an idealised but impoverished rural Bengal.

In 1901 Tagore moved to *Shantiniketan* (Abode of Peace) where he established an *ashram* with a marble-floored prayer hall, an experimental school, gardens, and a library. He financed this institution with his book royalties of around 2,000 rupees in those days and the monthly payments he received as part of his inheritance. Later he sold his family's jewellery and his seaside bungalow in Puri (Odisha) and ploughed all proceeds in this venture where teaching was often conducted under trees.

Tagore personally took classes in the mornings and wrote textbooks in the afternoons. He named the institution Vishwa-*Bharati* (India in the World) and vowed to "make Santiniketan the connecting thread between India and the world

[and] a world centre for the study of humanity somewhere beyond the limits of nation and geography."

By 1939, *Vishwa Bharti* had become a full-fledged university. It soon became one of India's most renowned places for higher learning. It produced alumni such as Indira Gandhi (later Prime Minister of India), Amartya Sen (Nobel Laureate) and Satyajit Ray (award-winning film director). After India's independence, Government of India adopted this experimental university and is still funding it fully.

Tagore wrote the *Gitanjali* (Song Offerings), a collection of 157 poems that became famous for its "*profoundly sensitive, fresh and beautiful verse.*" Some 53 of these poems were translated into English, which spread his fame across continents.

In translation his poetry was viewed as spiritual and mercurial. Even though experts assert that no one who can read Tagore's poems in Bengali can feel satisfied with any of the translations (made with or without Yeats's help). E.M. Forster too has noted that "*the theme is so beautiful,*" but the charms have "*vanished in translation,*" or perhaps "*in an experiment that has not quite come off.*"

The Swedish Academy, however, was so impressed with the idealistic nature of his poetry that it awarded him the Noble prize for literature in 1913. This created history by making him the first non-European to get this prestigious award.

Note: Shockingly on 25 March 2004, Tagore's Nobel Prize was reported missing from the safety vault of the Vishwa-Bharati University. The Swedish Academy, however, decided to replace these with two replicas of Tagore's Nobel Prize, one made of gold and the other of bronze, on 7 December 2004.

In the early 1930s, Tagore campaigned relentlessly against the widely prevalent "abnormal caste consciousness" and untouchability. His work *Chandalika* (Untouchable Girl), described how Monk Ananda, Gautama Buddha's disciple, asked a tribal girl for water, without caring for the girl's caste. He wrote poems and plays on Dalit heroes and campaigned—successfully—to open many temples like the famous Guruvayoor to the downtrodden.

In *Chokher Bali* (directed later as a film by Satyajit Ray) Tagore inscribed Bengali society through the eyes of a rebellious young widow who preferred to live alone. In doing so, he boldly pilloried the custom of perpetual mourning for widows, and questioned why they were not allowed to remarry.

Tagore was a prolific composer with 2,230 songs to his credit. His songs are known as *rabindrasangit* (Tagore Music). They are so popular that even today there "*is in Bengal no cultured home where Rabindranath's songs are not sung or at least attempted to be sung ... Even illiterate villagers sing his songs.*"

His songs impacted the Bengali ethos in the same manner as Shakespeare had impacted the English-speaking world. These songs "*transcend the mundane to the aesthetic and express all ranges and categories of human emotion.*"

The poet gave voice to all—big or small, rich or poor. The poor Ganges boatman and the rich landlord, all aired their emotions in them. His influence was so profound that it left a deep imprint on the sitar maestro Vilayat Khan and sarod maestros Buddhadev Dasgupta and Amjad Ali Khan.

Tagore was deeply saddened by the partition of Bengal on communal lines in 1905. He saw this British move as an attempt to thwart India's National Movement by dividing Hindus and

Muslims. He wrote a song "*Amar Shona Bangla*" to inspire and unite all Bengalis and to protest against this divisive policy. This song became the national anthem of Bangladesh when it became an independent country in 1971.

Tagore wrote "*Jana Gana Mana*" in shadhu-bhasha, a Sanskritised version of Bengali. It was first sung in 1911 at a Calcutta session of the Indian National Congress. It became so popular that in 1950 the Constituent Assembly of the Republic of India adopted it as India's national anthem.

Tagore wrote eight novels and four novellas. His themes revolved around Indian nationalism, *Swadeshi* (indigenous) movement, religious zeal, exploitation of the poor, terrorism, etc. Tagore also wrote 84 short stories, which revolved around modernity, fashion and mind puzzles. Many of his novels were given renewed attention via film adaptations by Satyajit Ray and others.

"*For the world he became the voice of India's spiritual heritage; and for India, especially for Bengal, he became a great living institution.*"

Tagore had tried his hand at drawing when he was nearing forty and was already a celebrated writer. As he shared with the noted scientist Jagadishchandra Bose,

"*You will be surprised to hear that I am sitting with a sketchbook drawing. Needless to say, the pictures are not intended for any salon in Paris, they cause me not the least suspicion that the national gallery of any country will suddenly decide to raise taxes to acquire them. But, just as a mother lavishes most affection on her ugliest son, so I feel secretly drawn to the very skill that comes to me least easily.*"

However, by sixty, Tagore had taken up drawing and painting again with full gusto. His paintings appeared in many exhibitions in Paris and throughout Europe. Interestingly, he was colour blind which resulted in him using strange colour schemes and displaying unusual aesthetics.

Tagore was a "peripatetic litterateur" who roamed around the world affirming his belief in the oneness of that humanity. On 14 July 1927 Tagore and two companions began a four-month tour of Southeast Asia.

In his other travels, Tagore interacted with Henri Bergson, Albert Einstein, Robert Frost, Thomas Mann, George Bernard Shaw, H.G. Wells, and Romain Rolland. In May 1926 Tagore met Mussolini in Rome. He was warmly received but Tagore couldn't help pronouncing against the dictator's fascist policies.

His visits to Persia and Iraq (in 1932) and Sri Lanka (in 1933) only deepened Tagore's dislike of communalism and nationalism. Tagore was a man ahead of his time. He wrote in 1932, while on a visit to Iran, that "*each country of Asia will solve its own historical problems according to its strength, nature and needs, but the lamp they will each carry on their path to progress will converge to illuminate the common ray of knowledge.*"

He recounted how during a May 1932 visit to a Bedouin encampment in the Iraqi desert, the tribal chief told him that "*Our prophet has said that a true Muslim is he by whose words and deeds not the least of his brother-men may ever come to any harm ...*"

Tagore recorded in his diary that, "*I was startled into recognising in his words the voice of essential humanity.*"

His travelogues, essays, and lectures were compiled into several volumes, including *Europe Jatrir Patro* (Letters from

Europe) and *Manusher Dhormo* (The Religion of Man). His brief chat with Einstein, "Note on the Nature of Reality," is included as an appendix to the latter.

Tagore supported the Indian freedom movement and wrote songs lionising it. Two of his compositions, "*Chitto Jetha Bhayshunyo*" ("Where the Mind is Without Fear") and "*Ekla Chalo Re*" ("If They Answer Not to Thy Call, Walk Alone"), gained mass appeal, with the latter becoming Gandhi's favourite.

Yet in an acerbic 1925 essay he lampooned the Swadeshi movement as "The Cult of the Charka," or the spinning wheel that Mahatma Gandhi was so fond of. He suggested that Indians avoid the victim mentality and instead improve their lot through self-help and education. Tagore saw the presence of the British in India as a "political symptom of our social disease." He maintained that, even for the extremely poor "steady and purposeful education" was better than "blind revolution."

In 1934, an earthquake hit Bihar and killed thousands. Gandhi hailed it as divine retribution avenging the oppression of the untouchables. Tagore rebuked him publically for such insensitive remarks because the disaster had actually killed more poor people than upper caste ones.

Later, however, he mediated in a Gandhi–Ambedkar dispute regarding separate electorates for untouchables. Gandhi in protest had gone on a fast unto death, and Tagore had to persuade Ambedkar to drop this rather divisive demand, thereby making Gandhi end his fast.

Tagore's charms appear to ascend the barriers of time and place. An astonished Salman Rushdie recently reported a latent reverence for Tagore of all places in Nicaragua.

Even today, many events around the world pay tribute to Tagore every year. His birth anniversary *Kabipranam* (Salutations to the poet) is regularly celebrated by the annual Tagore Festival held in Urbana, Illinois (USA). Then there is the *Rabindra Path Parikrama*, which is a walking pilgrimage from Kolkata to Shantiniketan.

In 2011, to celebrate the 150th birth anniversary of Tagore, Harvard University Press collaborated with *Vishwa-Bharati* University to publish *The Essential Tagore*, the largest anthology of Tagore's works available in English.

There are very few artists in the world who are good at everything. Either you are a painter or a musician or a novelist or an actor....

I can only think of Leonardo Da Vinci as someone who could do almost everything. The second example could be Tagore.

Incidentally both Rabindranath Tagora and Da Vinci were quiet artists.

The lesson then is: If you have ever felt that you are good at many things, why hold yourself back. Be your own Tagore or Da Vinci.

And be proud of the fact that you are an introvert.

"Who are you, reader, reading my poems a hundred years hence?

I cannot send you one single flower from this wealth of the spring, one single streak of gold from yonder clouds.

Open your doors and look abroad..........

The water in a vessel is sparkling; the water in the sea is dark.

The small truth has words which are clear; the great truth has great silence."

–Rabindranath Tagore

Chapter 8: A Suicidal, Body Mutilating, Drug Addict Refuses to Audition and Becomes the Highest Paid Hollywood Superstar in History

She walked on the red carpet in a shimmering YSL black dress that in her signature style blended androgyny with sex appeal. Her green eyes, considered the most beautiful among any female celebrity, were dazzling. Her dark brown hair was open and flowing free.

Ms. Voight had been the highest paid actress in Hollywood for five years in a row. People presumed that she had it easy; so easy that she could afford to indulge in a lot of "unpleasant activities" in her teens.

Did that make her undeserving of public adulation, admiration, respect or recognition?

In one of her interviews, she said:

"*Like many of the greatest human stories, it is about the capacity of regular men and women to rise above adversity. It reminds us never to give up, and that having the spirit to fight is what really matters. It is powerful because it speaks to the potential inside all of us ... I do believe in the old saying 'What does not kill you makes you stronger.' Our experiences, good and bad, make us who we are. By overcoming difficulties, we gain strength and maturity."*

So who is this Ms. Voight and why are we talking about her?

Let us start at the beginning.

Ms. Voight was born into a well-known family in Hollywood. Her father John Voight was an Oscar winning actor. However, he was unfaithful to his wife, which in due course resulted in divorce.

Ms. Voight's childhood was then anything but happy. She was raised by her single mother who struggled to make ends meet. Ms. Voight craved for love and affection. School was no respite where other students teased her for being thin and for wearing glasses and braces.

Her mother tried to make her take modeling assignments, but that didn't work out. Ms. Voight then shifted to an alternative school where she became a "punk outsider," wearing all-black clothing, and experimenting with knife play. She now wanted to be a funeral director and started to study embalming.

Recapitulating that tumultuous period, she says, "*I am still at heart—and always will be—just a punk kid with tattoos.*"

As a teenager, the young Ms. Voight found it difficult to connect with other people, and started to harm herself. As she admitted later, "*For some reason, the ritual of having cut myself and feeling the pain, maybe feeling alive, feeling some kind of release, it was somehow therapeutic to me.*"

The anger and frustration she felt led her to dark and sinister thoughts. She often thought of committing suicide. She once even hired a hit man to kill her!

Ms. Voight had trouble falling asleep at night. So she began experimenting with drugs. By the age of 20, she had used "just about every drug possible" and the list included cocaine, ecstasy, LSD and heroine. At the age of 24, she suffered a nervous breakdown and spent 72 hours in the UCLA Medical Centre's Psychiatric Ward.

Ms. Voight had first acted in a movie in 1982, when she was seven, alongside her father, Jon Voight. However, she could make up her mind to take up acting as a profession only at the age of 16. But there was a serious hitch: she just couldn't pass auditions.

She was often told that her demeanour was "too dark." In between her battles with drug addiction, Ms. Voight worked on her acting skills. She got admitted to the Lee Strasberg Theatre Institute where she trained for two years and acted in a few plays.

Getting past auditions was no problem now. In a 1993 movie, she was selected to play the leading role of a humanoid designed for corporate espionage and assassination. The movie, however, bombed at the box office.

Ms. Voight was so shattered that she refused to audition for almost a year. After a while, she gathered courage to play the role of a vagabond who united teenage girls against a teacher who was harassing them sexually. A critic commented that it took a lot of hogwash to develop such a character but it was creditable that Ms. Voight had the presence to overcome the stereotype.

By 1997, just four years later, Ms. Voight's career took an interesting turn. Her role of Cornelia Wallace, the second wife of the segregationist Alabama Governor and presidential candidate, in the movie *George Wallace* (1997) fetched her a Golden Globe award. Critics considered her performance as the highlight of the film. People began to notice her not just as Jon Voight's daughter, but as a talented actor in her own right.

There was no looking back thereafter. Ms. Voight was now an unstoppable juggernaut playing all kinds of roles in numerous films. She was noticed for her charm and sharp features and she started creating a name for herself.

Ms. Voight's dedication to her roles was legendary. While shooting for a film, that got her the Golden Globe Award, she immersed herself so much in the role that she told her husband that she would not be able to phone him: "*I'd tell him: I'm alone; I'm dying; I'm gay; I'm not going to see you for weeks.*"

Then came her breakthrough moment. In 2001, she performed the role of an archaeologist adventurer in a movie which was an adaptation of a popular video game. The role required her to master an English accent and undergo extensive martial arts training. The film was an international success, earning $274.7 million worldwide, and establishing Ms. Voight's global reputation as a female superstar. Fans were gaga over her unconventional looks, which was credited to a mixture of German and Slovak descent on her father's side, and of French-Canadian, Dutch, and German ancestry on her mother's side.

The movie also established Ms. Voight among Hollywood's highest-paid actresses, earning $10–$15 million per film for the next five years.

I'm sure you would have guessed by now the identity of this mysterious Ms. Voight.

She is—the gorgeous **Angelina Jolie.** And the movie was **Lara Croft: Tomb Raider**.

And yes, she never used the name of Ms. Voight to identify herself. Jolie in fact formally petitioned a court to remove her surname "Voight" in favour of her middle name. This was granted to her on September 12, 2002.

Angelina's intense on-screen persona may make you think that she is very fierce, outspoken, bold and, therefore, an extrovert. She has been labelled as "*one of the great wild spirits of current movies, a loose cannon who somehow has a deadly aim.*"

However, reality is somewhat different. In a 2005 interview, Angelina revealed her quiet side. She admitted that she loved to spend a lot of time by herself as it helped her develop as a person. She also confessed that she does not follow the crowd and likes to meet new people on her own terms.

"*I don't have a lot of friends. I've been alone a lot. You know what it is? I think when you're alone, when you go someplace and you're by yourself, you end up meeting new people and you develop,*" she said.

Yes, she had a dark past. She had a wild phase as well. On March 28, 1996, she attended her wedding (with her first husband) in black rubber pants and a white T-shirt, upon which she had written the groom's name in her blood! Later, she along with her second husband took to wearing each other's blood in a tiny vial around their necks!

Among her estimated 17 tattoos are the Latin proverb "*quod me nutrit me destruit*" (what nourishes me destroys me), the Tennessee Williams quote "*A prayer for the wild at heart, kept in cages,*" a Buddhist Sanskrit prayer of protection, a twelve-inch tiger, and geographical coordinates indicating the birthplaces of her children. She recently showed off three new tattoos on her back while directing her Khmer Rouge film "*First They Killed My Father*" in Cambodia.

Angelina would often do things that made her look more like a failure than a success. But she also had the determination to channelise all her anger, frustration, pain and suffering to portray such complex characters on screen that made her performances memorable. From a robot to a sociopath, a vagabond to a female martial warrior, a grief stricken widow in Pakistan (*A Mighty Heart,* 2007) to a witch in "*Maleficent*" (2014), she had a blast essaying all kinds of roles. In doing that she has proved that ultimately it's what we do and how we channelise our negative energy is what turns us in to a success or a failure.

At the personal level, after two failed marriages, that lasted three years each, Angelina seems to be settling down with Brad Pitt, another Hollywood celebrity. They have been together since 2005 and got married on August 23, 2014. Brangelina, as the celebrity press calls them, has had six children, of which three are adopted from war-torn regions.

Her adopted children come from Cambodia, Ethiopia, and Vietnam. It was her way of undoing years of self-inflicted harm. The message is: Love others if you have ever wronged hating yourself. After adopting her first child from Cambodia, Jolie said that she found stability in her life, adding that, "*I knew once I committed to Maddox, I would never be self-destructive again.*"

She recently cast three of her children—Vivienne, Pax, and Zahara (whom she calls ZZ)—in her 2014 film "Maleficent." As she explains,

"*Brad and I made the decision that we wouldn't keep them from sets and the fun of making movies, but we wouldn't [glorify it either]—we wouldn't make it a good thing or a bad thing.*"

"But I would really prefer they do something else. [Anyway] after two days of it, Brad and I were so stressed we never wanted to do it again," she joked.

To connect her adopted son with his roots, Jolie purchased a house in Cambodia in 2003. She later bought 60,000 hectares in the adjacent Samlout National Park in the Cardamom Mountains and turned the area into a wildlife reserve. In recognition of her conservation efforts, the Cambodian King Norodom Sihamoni awarded her Cambodian citizenship on July 31, 2005.

In December 2010, Jolie along with Brad Pitt, established in the name of their Namibian-born daughter the Shiloh Jolie-Pitt Foundation. This supports conservation projects as well as a free health clinic, housing, and a school for the San Bushmen community in the Naankuse Wildlife Sanctuary, in the Kalahari. The couple have been quite fond of this place from the time they had travelled to Namibia for the birth of their first biological child in 2006.

Their aim then was to just avoid the paparazzi. But later, they decided to sell the first pictures of Shiloh through Getty Images to the magazines "People" and "Hello!" for $4.1 and $3.5 million respectively. This was a record sum for celebrity photojournalism in those days, which they promptly donated to UNICEF.

In Sebeta, Ethiopia, the birthplace of her eldest (adopted) daughter, Angelina has set up the Zahara Children's Center. This treats and educates children suffering from HIV or tuberculosis.

Angelina Jolie was always considered a rebel. She supports having guns stating *"she had no problem defending their family and home with a firearm."*

And then, she did something that was till then considered unthinkable for any celebrity of her class.

On February 16, 2013, a 37-year old Angelina underwent a preventive double mastectomy. She took this decision after learning that she carried a defective BRCA1 gene that indicated an 87% risk of developing breast cancer.

The chattering classes were aghast. Was Angelina again displaying her self-mutilating streak? After all, she didn't yet have the cancer. And even if she had, the latest advances in medical science could certainly provide her much better treatment than what could be provided to her mother who suffered from breast cancer and who died from ovarian cancer.

But Angelina was adamant. Mastectomy would have brought down her chances of developing breast cancer from 87% to less than 5%. So she went ahead with the operation and subsequent reconstructive surgery involving implants and grafts.

But this wasn't the end of Angelina's medical travails. Just two years later, in March 2015, Angelina decided to have a preventive oophorectomy, as she had a 50% risk of developing ovarian cancer due to the same genetic anomaly.

The thing to note, however, is that Angelina, who is otherwise an intensely private person, decided to go public about her motivations. She discussed her diagnosis, surgeries, and personal experiences in considerable detail in "The New York Times." She said that she took this proactive measure for the sake of her six children, and explained,

"I choose not to keep my story private because there are many women who do not know that they might be living under the shadow of cancer. It is my hope that they, too, will be able to get gene

tested, and that if they have a high risk they, too, will know that they have strong options."

She also added that, "*On a personal note, I do not feel any less of a woman. I feel empowered that I made a strong choice that in no way diminishes my femininity.*"

The public figure that Angelina is, her operations raised tremendous awareness of BRCA mutations and the options available to at-risk women. In, what the TIME magazine called, "The Angelina Effect," the number of referrals tripled in Australia, doubled in the UK, parts of Canada, and India, and significantly increased in the U.S.

There was a positive effect also on reducing the costs of gene testing when the U.S. Supreme Court, in a June 2013 ruling, invalidated BRCA gene patents held by the company Myriad Genetics.

In a change of track, Angelina Jolie now wants to be a director rather than an actor. She has already directed the Second World War survival drama "*Unbroken*" in 2010 and a Bosnian war film "*In the Land of Blood and Honey*" in 2011. For the latter, Jolie was named an honorary citizen of Sarajevo.

Angelina's third directorial effort was the marital drama "By the Sea" (2015), in which she starred opposite her husband, Brad Pitt.

As she explains, she prefers being out of the spotlight and feels that directing films is a great way to lose her massive celebrity status.

"*I'm a very private person,*" declares Angelina, adding that, "*I don't go out much. I'm home with kids. I go to work. I don't really like being the focus of attention, which is why I like being behind the camera more.*"

Specifically on directing, she says,

"I prefer directing to acting. There is huge freedom that comes from being behind the camera. It brings a lot of responsibilities as well, but is intensely rewarding. Particularly the chance to help draw out the best in young actors, like Jack O'Connell in Unbroken, who is a remarkable talent."

She told "Interview" magazine, "*My mom always wanted me to be an actor. And I started going to theatre and going on auditions young. I only realised about five years ago that I actually didn't want to be an actor...... I never knew the other. I grew up with my career being thrust upon me. It took me a long time to believe that I could do more than that one aspect of our business.*"

Jolie had several awards and accolades showered over her. She has received an Academy Award, two Screen Actors Guild Awards, and three Golden Globe Awards. She won the Oscar for the Best Supporting Actress for her performance in the movie "*Girl, Interrupted*" (1999).

Angelina is equally well-noted for her humanitarian efforts. In November 2013, she received a Jean Hersholt Humanitarian Award, which is an honorary Award from the Board of Governors of the Academy of Motion Picture Arts and Sciences. In 2014, Queen Elizabeth II presented her the insignia of an Honorary Dame Commander of the Order of St. Michael and St. George (DCMG) for campaigning to end sexual violence in war zones and for her services to the UK's foreign policy.

Angelina was twice in 2006 and 2008 included in the Time 100 list of the most influential people in the world. Forbes's Celebrity 100 issue in 2009 named her as the world's most powerful actress from 2006 to 2008 and 2011 to 2013. In addition, Forbes declared her as Hollywood's highest-paid actress in 2009, 2011, and 2013, with estimated annual earnings of $27 million, $30 million, and $33 million respectively. A 2015 global survey conducted by *YouGov* found Angelina to be the most admired woman in the world.

Angelina has been very generous in sharing her wealth with the downtrodden. Without thinking twice, she donated $1 million in response to an international UNHCR emergency appeal. This is the largest donation UNHCR had ever received from a private individual. No wonder, she is also the longest serving Goodwill Ambassador for the United Nations High Commission for Refugees, a responsibility that she accepted in 2001.

Angelina makes it a point to cover scrupulously all costs related to her humanitarian missions. She also shares the same rudimentary working and living conditions as other UNHCR field staff on all her visits. The tireless person she is, she began taking flying lessons in 2004 to help ferry aid workers and food supplies around the world. And she now proudly holds a pilot's license.

So what is remarkable is that despite all adversities and questionable decisions, romantic or otherwise, she has learnt from each of her mistakes, has persevered and achieved excellence. Today she is admired as an intelligent, charming, compassionate and a bold woman. She's one of the few celebrities to look up to because of her indomitable spirit and what she goes on to accomplish with it.

"Without pain, there would be no suffering, without suffering we would never learn from our mistakes. To make it right, pain and suffering is the key to all windows, without it, there is no way of life."

"If you don't get out of the box you've been raised in, you won't understand how much bigger the world is."

–Angelina Jolie

Chapter 9: Learn From Leonardo

Are you a creative person with so many diverse passions that people sometimes call you "confused?"

Don't worry then my friend because I feel the same.

By training, I am a corporate lawyer. But by profession, I am a writer. In which genre, fiction or non-fiction......please don't ask.

Because the few years that I have been in "business," I have written over 17 books (this one is the 18th) in genres ranging from cookbooks to self-help, introversion to publishing and memoirs to fiction. In the coming years, I may feel adventurous enough to experiment with adventure or a few more genres like fantasy or thriller.

Sensible and experienced business veterans may tut-tut and say that such "fickle-minded" behaviour makes little sense. That you need to always play to your strengths. That by dabbling in so many sectors you will only fritter away your energies. That financially so many trickles will never become a torrent.....

If like me, you don't agree, then just quote one example and that should shut every one fast. And that artist, is the brilliant, the great, the one and only—**Leonardo Da Vinci**.

Born on April 15, 1452, in Vinci, Italy, Leonardo's father Ser Piero was a prominent attorney notary. His mother was a poor peasant girl who had given birth to Leonard out of wedlock.

Despite not receiving much of a formal education, Leonardo turned out to be perhaps one of the most diversely talented people who ever walked on the planet Earth. Unable to "cope with only one skill," he became an artist, painter, sculptor, inventor, mathematician, engineer, architect, anatomist and writer. And that was not all.

He was also a story teller, joke teller, riddle-designer, and a prankster. Leonardo was ambidextrous and could write and paint with both hands at the same time. He was labelled as a "polymath," which meant that he was "addicted" to doing TOO many things at the same time!

While no one in his right mind can suggest that anyone can become Leonardo Da Vinci overnight (or perhaps even in his/her lifetime), there are a few things everyone can learn from him.

First, that Leonardo did not master all of his skills over one fine weekend. He did them one at a time. He had multiple interests in multiple fields because fortunately there was no push to specialise in those days.

But Leonardo didn't differentiate between subjects because he believed that they were all inter-related. The learning and discoveries made in one area, he believed, affected your understanding of another subject or branch of study. As he declared:

"Nothing can be loved or hated unless it is first understood."

At 14, recognising his potential as an artist, Leonardo's father sent him to attend a workshop owned by the famous sculptor and painter of the time, Andrea Del Verrocchio of Florence. During this apprenticeship, Leonardo met other trainees who were knowledgeable in chemistry, mechanics and the other technical skills. This fuelled his curiosity to understand nature.

Soon Leonardo was outshining his teacher. At 20, he was accepted into the Painters' Guild of Florence. This brought him fame overnight and gave him access to the most powerful people in Italy.

Leonardo's rather unusual interest in human anatomy, skeleton and body parts took his painting techniques to a new level. His knowledge of anatomy helped him to create stunning life-like portraits. These were filled for the first time with emotions of intrigue, feelings and inner states of mind. His most famous examples are the *Mona Lisa* and the *Vitruvian Man*.

Da Vinci was product of an era that began a new way of thinking. When people were seeking freedom from dogmatic inflexible traditions. When imagination flourished and artists were thought to be near divine beings. When Europe was emerging out of a period of darkness and confusion. And when the sunshine of the Renaissance period was enveloping everyone in its warm embrace.

Still it was incredibly rare for an illegitimate child with no formal education to rise above his natural born status. And become an established household name and a revered artist.

Leonardo's natural curiosity led him to produce many scientific journals. His interest in engineering led him to create musical instruments, drawings of planes, steam ships, hydraulic pumps, cannons and war machines. Experts believe that the battle tanks used in the First World War were inspired by the designs of Leonardo's war machines, which he had drawn some four hundred years earlier.

So the takeaway is that if you too have multiple skills, like Leonardo Da Vinci, you may want to think of using one set of skills to improve the other. For example, if you love to blog regularly, why not consider writing a full book? Or why not create on-line courses when you love teaching and mentoring. Or become a professional chef because you love cooking. Or create new video games or mobile apps because you love playing video games. Or become a professional actor because you love mimicking and being someone else for some time. The possibilities could just be endless.

And yes, if you monetised any of your special talents in this manner, no one will certainly call you "confused!"

Now to the question: Was Leonardo Da Vinci a quiet artist?

Leonard's contemporaries have described his personality as charming, graceful yet reserved. He valued solitude, and his views below strongly attest to his introversion:

"If you are alone you belong entirely to yourself. If you are accompanied by even one companion you belong only half to yourself or even less in proportion to the thoughtlessness of his conduct and if you have more than one companion you will fall more deeply into the same plight."

As a fellow introvert, I can relate to this quotation instantly. It feels as if Leonardo is speaking for every introvert on this planet. So there is no doubt that Da Vinci was an introvert.

It was only when he was alone that he could be creative and could dabble with his wide range of interests, skills and specialisations. If it wasn't for solitude, *Mona Lisa* wouldn't be born. *Vitruvian Man* would not have been created. The *Last Supper* wouldn't have been painted. And tanks, helicopters, hydraulic pumps, bicycles and even contact lenses could not have been designed.

Leonardo was also very humble:

"I have offended God and mankind because my work didn't reach the quality it should have."

But do learn from him to keep things simple because in Leonardo's words:

"Simplicity is the ultimate sophistication."

And if you are having difficulty in starting something new and exciting, here is another gem from him:

"It's easier to resist at the beginning than at the end."

Da Vinci is a great example to follow except for a few negatives. He was a restless artist who abandoned many of his projects mid-way. In 1478, he took on his first commissioned work for Florence's San Donato monastery. Without finishing this assignment he went away to Milan to serve the ruling Sforza dynasty. There he worked on a bronze equestrian statue for 12 years, but never completed it.

Even the "*Mona Lisa*," which some historians argue was his greatest artistic achievement, was never "completed." The painting is believed to depict Lisa Del Gioconda, wife of Francesco Del Giocondo, a wealthy silk merchant who had commissioned it to commemorate the birth of their second child. The painting is dated between 1505 and 1507, but there are indications that Leonardo continued to work on it as he tried to achieve perfection. So the work was never delivered to Gioconda and is now housed behind bullet proof glass in Louvre, Paris!

It appears that Leonardo's quest for perfection sometimes meant that he would lose his passion for the work in hand mid-way and turn his genius towards something completely different. It looks like he may have been distracted by too many of his interests and passions at the same time. This caused great frustration for the kings and the paymasters of those days. Quite a classic example of how perfection and distraction can harm your projects.

The most important lesson, therefore, would be to prefer completion over perfection—to finish what you start.

Naturally Leonardo's brilliant artistic patronage couldn't continue unbroken. He knew he needed to move in the right circles and even become a member of the famous Italian guilds to succeed in life. And he succeeded in hitting a mark and was given assignment after assignment.

But once the regime changed hands, so did his patronage. As a result, many times Leonardo's source of income dried up. It is said that he left Milan as a broken man, abandoning his *Last Supper* masterpiece and many other famous works.

The lesson: Make sure you have contingency plans or safety nets in place.

Do plan to have multiple streams of income. Earmark enough investments in ultra-safe instruments to work as an emergency fund that could help put food on your table at least for six months. Do establish a formidable reputation in the industry you work. And finally, try to take on more than a few clients. So that if one fails, the others continue to pay you.

Da Vinci left for France from Italy in 1516 upon receiving an appointment from Francis I, the King of France. The offer included his stay at Château of Cloux, a country house near Aboise, France and the chance to paint and draw at his own pace.

However, he could spend just three years in France and died shortly after his 67th birthday on May 2, 1519.

Leonardo's abiding message was that if you have multiple series of passions, don't think of it as a burden, but as a gift that few possess. So take great pride in it. And celebrate it.

It was only because of this gift that Da Vinci could rise from poverty to prosperity and became a legend in his own lifetime. For creative thinkers everywhere, he is an awe-inspiring model. Perhaps he can help YOU too to achieve unrivalled brilliance and outstanding creativity.

"I have been impressed with the urgency of doing. Knowing is not enough; we must apply. Being willing is not enough; we must do."

–Leonardo Da Vinci

Books by Prasenjeet Kumar in the Quiet Phoenix Series

CELEBRATING QUIET PEOPLE: UPLIFTING STORIES FOR INTROVERTS AND HIGHLY SENSITIVE PERSONS

QUIET PHOENIX: AN INTROVERT'S GUIDE TO RISING IN CAREER & LIFE

QUIET PHOENIX 2: FROM FAILURE TO FULFILMENT: A MEMOIR OF AN INTROVERTED CHILD

CELEBRATING QUIET LEADERS: UPLIFTING STORIES OF INTROVERTED LEADERS WHO CHANGED HISTORY

CELEBRATING QUIET ARTISTS: STIRRING STORIES OF INTROVERTED ARTISTS THE WORLD CAN'T FORGET

FICTION by Prasenjeet Kumar

THE MURDER OF MR. SACHDEVA

THE FORBIDDEN TRUTH: SEASON ONE

THE FORBIDDEN TRUTH: SEASON TWO

THE FORBIDDEN TRUTH: SEASON FINALE

LEGALLY IN LOVE

LOVE KARMA CROSSED

WHEN GANGES MET THE NORTH SEA

YOU CAN'T KILL MY LOVE: A KASHMIR HOLOCAUST LOVE STORY

AUTISTICALLY YOURS

STILL MISSING...

WHEN YOU CAN'T TRUST LOVE

THE ENEMY WITHIN

THE SCEPTIC

FICTION by Arun Kumar and Prasenjeet Kumar

KASHMIR IS FREE

KASHMIR THINKS ITS FREE

KASHMIR IS FREE FINALLY

Books by Prasenjeet Kumar in the "Self-Publishing WITHOUT SPENDING A DIME" Series

HOW TO BE AN AUTHOR ENTREPRENEUR WITHOUT SPENDING A DIME

HOW TO TRANSLATE YOUR BOOKS WITHOUT SPENDING A DIME

HOW TO MARKET YOUR BOOKS WITHOUT SPENDING A DIME

HOW TO HAVE A HAPPIER WRITER MINDSET WITHOUT SPENDING A DIME

Cookbooks by Prasenjeet Kumar (with Sonali Kumar)

HOME STYLE INDIAN COOKING IN A JIFFY

HOW TO COOK IN A JIFFY EVEN IF YOU HAVE NEVER BOILED AN EGG BEFORE

HEALTHY COOKING IN A JIFFY: THE COMPLETE NO FAD NO DIET HANDBOOK

HOW TO CREATE A COMPLETE MEAL IN A JIFFY

THE ULTIMATE GUIDE TO COOKING LENTILS THE INDIAN WAY

THE ULTIMATE GUIDE TO COOKING RICE THE INDIAN WAY

THE ULTIMATE GUIDE TO COOKING FISH THE INDIAN WAY

THE ULTIMATE GUIDE TO COOKING CHICKEN THE INDIAN WAY

THE ULTIMATE GUIDE TO COOKING VEGETABLES THE INDIAN WAY

THE ULTIMATE GUIDE TO COOKING DESSERTS THE INDIAN WAY

THE ULTIMATE INDIAN INSTANT POT COOKBOOK

Connect With the Author

Please do feel free to visit us at: http://publishwithprasen.com

Should you have any questions or comments, please do not hesitate to write to us anytime at: prasenjeet@publishwithprasen.com OR prasenpublishers@gmail.com.

We would also love to connect with you on social media.

Join us on:

Twitter

https://twitter.com/publishwithprasen

Goodreads

https://www.goodreads.com/prasenjeet

About The Author

Prasenjeet Kumar is the author/co-author of over 39 books in four genres: Fiction, motivational books for introverts (the Quiet Phoenix series), books on Self-Publishing (Self-Publishing WITHOUT SPENDING A DIME series) and cookbooks (Cooking In A Jiffy series). His books (over 100 titles and counting) have been translated into French, German, Italian, Japanese, Spanish, and Portuguese, and sell in over 50 countries.

Prasenjeet is a Law graduate from the University College London (2005-2008), London University and a Philosophy Honours graduate from St. Stephen's College (2002-2005), Delhi University. In addition, he holds a Legal Practice Course (LPC) Diploma from College of Law, Bloomsbury, London, and was for a brief while, a solicitor of England and Wales.

Prasenjeet loves gourmet food, music, films, and travelling. He has already covered thirty-six countries including Australia, Canada, China, Denmark, Dubai, Egypt, Estonia, Finland, France, Germany, Greece, Hong Kong, Iceland, Indonesia, Israel, Italy, Jordan, Latvia, Lithuania, Macau, Malaysia, Mauritius, Monaco, Montenegro, Nepal, New Zealand, Norway, Sharjah, Spain, Sweden, Switzerland, Thailand, Turkey, UK, Uzbekistan, and the USA.

Prasenjeet is the self-taught designer, writer, editor, and proud owner of the website cookinginajiffy.com which he has dedicated to his mother. He also runs another website publishwithprasen.com where he shares tips about writing and self-publishing.

9 788197 187933

Printed at Repro India Ltd.